Balanced Scorecards and Activity-Based Management

FINANCIAL TIMES
Management Briefings

Balanced Scorecards and Activity-Based Management

The practical application

JOHN SMULLEN

FT
PITMAN
PUBLISHING

London • Hong Kong • Johannesburg • Melbourne • Singapore • Washington DC

PITMAN PUBLISHING
128 Long Acre, London WC2E 9AN
Tel: +44 (0)171 447 2000
Fax: +44 (0)171 240 5771

A division of Pearson Professional Limited

First published in Great Britain 1997

ISBN 0 273 63265 5

British Library Cataloguing in Publication Data
A CIP catalogue record for this book can be obtained from the British Library.

10 9 8 7 6 5 4 3 2 1

Printed and bound in Great Britain

The Publishers' policy is to use paper manufactured from sustainable forests.

About the author

John Smullen, BSc, MA, MSc, MBA was educated at the London School of Economics, Birkbeck College and the London Business School. During the period 1973–86 he held a number of academic posts teaching economics.

He joined Abbey National Plc, the fifth largest bank in the United Kingdom, in 1986 to establish a linear programming system to analyse the efficiency of their branches. John Smullen was subsequently promoted into senior management and undertook a number of jobs developing delivery systems for financial management information. When he left in 1994 to set up his own consultancy, he was senior finance manager responsible for product, customer and organisational unit performance.

In 1994 he set up John Smullen Consultancy and Training which specialises in providing training and financial management information consultancy to the retail financial services industry. He is also a visiting lecturer in finance at the De Montfort University and Senior Academic Associate at the University of Greenwich.

He is a frequent contributor to banking industry conferences and has lectured on a diversity of finance related topics, including: branch evaluation; product development and evaluation; customer profitability; activity-based management; unit performance evaluation and bank pricing. He has lectured in Europe, the United States, the Middle East and Australia. John has published a number of articles on various financial topics in relation to banking and in October 1995 published a book entitled, *Financial Management Information and Analysis for Retail Banks* in conjunction with Woodhead Publishing and the Chartered Institute of Bankers.

I dedicate this book to Marion

CONTENTS

FOREWORD

History records that in the Roman Empire, where a Legion showed signs of cowardice one in ten among its ranks would be killed to encourage the others. This was known as decimation.

Those times may be long gone, but even today, in many organisations, when under pressure, they seek to reduce their cost base across all departments by, say 10 per cent on the basis that this is a 'fair' way of sharing the pain.

The fact that such a need exists at all, or that this approach is seen as the 'solution' often reflects the failures of past management to understand and respond successfully to the commercial environment in which the organisation operates.

The underlying thesis of this book is that if management has real understanding of what is happening in, and to, the business, then at least its decision-making will be well informed and it will be better able to avoid many of the mistakes of the past.

This sort of visibility comes through:

- monitoring the key measures of organisational performance
- understanding what drives the need for resources
- clear identification of the products, services and customers that generate, rather than erode, contribution.

Over recent years the disciplines of the balanced business scorecard and activity-based management have evolved to create this visibility in many organisations.

However, the full potential of these new techniques is only exploited fully when they are well understood by those who use them. The transition from implementation to action is often seriously under-estimated.

While the underlying principles of the balanced business scorecard and activity-based management are deceptively simple, there are still few books that readily communicate them to the reader. This one does.

This book is intended for those managers who:

- are relatively new to the balanced business scorecard and activity-based management
- want to understand what makes their business tick
- want to make a difference.

Unlike many, this book was written to be read and it forms a good introduction to the balanced business scorecard and activity-based management. It should serve you well.

Robin Bellis-Jones
Director
Develin & Partners
Management Consultants

PREFACE

The purpose of this book is to provide an introduction to the management accounting techniques of balanced scorecards and activity-based management. It gives an introduction to the ideas and the practical issues of implementing them within an organisation. My own experience in this field relates to the retail banking sector, and although I have drawn from that experience, the book is intended to be general in use and applicable to any organisational situation. This book is a brief introduction and although it considers what I consider to be the main practical issues of implementation it will not cover in detail all the practical issues presented by an implementation programme.

If one considers the introduction of any sophisticated management technique, there is no simple foolproof way to implement it. Balanced scorecards and activity-based management are not exceptions to this principle. Their value is only unlocked if they are implemented in a sensible and organisationally specific way. One certainly needs an overall vision of how to use the techniques and experience is useful in their implementation, but one must be aware that each situation is unique in terms of how the organisations intends to be successful, the activities which it undertakes and the nature of its internal politics. Effective introduction to an organisation requires subtlety, guile, understanding, imagination and energy, these qualities are needed in addition to any of the insights contained in the following chapters.

There are a great many people I would like to thank in the preparation of this book. They have conditioned my thoughts, eradicated my errors, worked and supported me and to them and many others I would like to extend my thanks, Robin Bellis-Jones, John Wriglesworth, David Meckin, Keith McDonald, Julie Mabberley,

Angela Zvesper, Nick Hand, Tim Murley, Shirley Edwards, Alan Swift, Ivor Jones, Sue Millar, Roger Haylock, Andy Jesson and David Withey. I would also like to thank my wife, Marion, who works so hard and deserves so much, and whose support is always powerful and present.

Part 1

The overview

1

The introduction

The key theme for business in the last few years have been the increasing levels of competition in all industries and markets. This new pressure is for many of a global nature. In the 1980s it was suggested that the remuneration of city dealers in London had to relate to that in New York and Tokyo. In *The Times* this weekend an economic commentator argued that the behaviour of the United States economy was now influenced by the fact that its blue collar workers competed with unskilled labour in the underdeveloped world. Therefore putting a limit on the degree to which there could be wage inflation in the US economy. This indicates the extent to which the world economy is becoming a single unit and the increased pressures on all businesses. The environment is not just one of enhanced competition but also one of greater uncertainty. Since the 1970s the economies of all the developed countries have become dramatically more volatile, this can be seen in terms of employment levels, interest rates and currency values. To this one can add the dramatically changing technology which has led to a revolution in the way that all businesses undertake their activities. It is difficult to believe that spreadsheets are less than 20 years old. Taking all these factors together there is much greater levels of risk involved in the undertaking of any business activity. The levels of risk faced by all individuals within our communities have also become much greater. In the face of these radical changes to the business environment there is a greater need for all enterprises to ensure that they use the best management techniques which are available to them.

In general the text uses words like business, firm, and enterprise to describe the units which are being considered. This is a matter of shorthand since the techniques can be applied to any organisation be it commercial, public sector or charity. Although there has been much controversy with the introduction of business techniques into the public sector and in particular the establishing of performance tables, it is my view that all these techniques can be applied generally. There may be some debate as to whether the correct techniques have been used in a particular instance or whether the specific application of the technique is sensitive and perceptive, but certainly I have no hesitation in believing the relevance of the techniques.

The central role in managing any business is dealing with the sheer volume of tasks that have to be undertaken and information which has to be processed. It is trying to organise the work process so that the management are controlling the enterprise rather than reacting to internally and externally generated crises. The two techniques which are the focus of this book, balanced scorecards and activity-based management, will greatly assist in the management of an enterprise, they are not the only techniques that an efficient firm should use but they have central value.

The management process can be understood, at its simplest level, in terms of Figure 1.1 which illustrates the relationship between objectives, activities and results. The business will have objectives and the management will try to achieve them by undertaking a number of activities, the set of reactions from within the firm and its environment will lead to a set of results. In order for the management to be effective it is important for it to understand the nature of the firm's objectives, the policy by which the firm intends to achieve its objectives, its relationship with its environment and how it is doing at any particular point in time. This is part of the process by which the management of a company can be integrated effectively in order to ensure they are all working towards the same goals in the same way.

Figure 1.1
AN OVERVIEW OF THE MANAGEMENT PROCESS

Objectives ⟶ Activities ⟶ Results

The implementation of a balanced scorecard and activity-based management within an organisation will provide a coherent framework in which to understand the relationship between objectives, activities and results and integrate the management process. It will focus the attention of management on that which is central to the success of the firm.

The balanced scorecard is a technique which will aid in the precise articulation of the organisation's objectives, the formulation of strategy, the generation of plans and budgets, and the setting up of an information system for performance monitoring and management. Its key essence is to establish a set of indicators for the performance of an organisation which will be more organisation specific and comprehensive than the standard set of financial indicators. They will, at the level of the organisation provide metrics for the management of the whole organisation and will focus on ensuring that the future performance of the organisation is guaranteed, rather than focusing on the past financial performance which is only an approximate indicator of the future performance. They will lead to a cascading set of indicators which will enable the units within the organisation to co-ordinate their targets and behaviour with the overall strategy of the organisation. It will focus all individuals within the organisation to implement its overall strategy and policy. The balanced scorecard is an attempt to establish a coherent management system for the enterprise.

Activity-based management (ABM) is a more traditional type of financial technique and many organisations had activity-based costing systems before the name became part of the accounting vocabulary. The key insight behind ABM is that costs within an organisation can only be justified in terms of the activities with which they are associated. If an activity is not valuable then it should not be undertaken and therefore any costs associated with it should be eliminated. The basis for ABM is an activity-based costing (ABC) exercise which relates the costs of an organisation to the activities which it undertakes. These costs can then be related to the key value generating relationships of the organisation termed cost objectives, namely organisational units, customers, products and processes. The strategy, policy and performance of the organisation can thus be better understood since the essence of ABC is to better understand what factors determine costs and how they can be influenced. Although ABC focuses on the cost structure, it is necessary to include some modelling of the revenue structure for ABM to generate its greatest benefits. Having set up an ABC model this can be used to understand the implications of strategy and policy, be the basis for cost reduction programmes and underlie the whole decisionmaking, budgetary and planning process. A better understanding of costs can lead automatically to better policy.

Although I would recommend these techniques to most organisations without reservation, it is important to understand that their worth depends on the way in which they are implemented. It is quite easy to introduce these techniques and for the management of the organisation to poorly implement them, it is also the case that they can be ignored within an organisation. They must be seen as crucial to the organisation and its management if they are to be successful.

2

Organisational management

The relationship between management information and the management process of an organisation should be very close. However, it is a common theme in most organisations that the information available is not that required, and the information that *is* required is not available. There is an aspect of inevitability about this perception since it is in the nature of management that as soon as one has extra or new information it allows us to ask better questions and this will require the development of new information systems.

The key to these new techniques is that they enable the creation of management information which is central to both the formulation of strategy and policy and the implementation of those strategies and policies. Considering the role of the management accountant, they should provide information which enables the organisation to identify its objectives and strategy, understand its current situation, understand the implications of its actions and ensure that all the different parts of the organisation have a coherent policy which is dedicated to fulfilling its objectives. If the techniques of balanced scorecards and activity-based management are implemented they will give extra sharpness to the organisation's management accounting system and the resulting management of the organisation.

Considering Figure 2.1, which elaborates on Figure 1.1, the workings of an organisation can be summarised in terms of objectives, strategy, implementation, the environmental reaction and the outcome. Taking each of these and considering them separately:

Figure 2.1
THE MANAGEMENT PROCESS OF THE ORGANISATION

Objectives ⟶ Strategy ⟶ Implementation ⟶ Environment ⟶ Results

OBJECTIVES

As was outlined in the first chapter the organisations to which these techniques can fruitfully be applied are not just commercial organisations. They would be just as useful for non-profit-making organisations like government departments, local authorities, quangos and charities, since all these organisations are interested in ensuring that they use their resources efficiently and that the actions of their personnel are directed towards fulfilling their organisational goals. In writing my book on *Financial Management Information and Analysis for Retail Banks* I identified a number of issues which are likely to be central to the focus of any public company; profitability, organisational value, risk and legal constraints. Profitability has been the traditional objective of many companies but the development of research in the United States notably by Alfred Rappaport has led many companies to set their targets in terms of shareholder value. This leads enterprises to focus on creating present value on their cashflows. This view is held by most large US corporates and is increasingly determining policy for companies in the United Kingdom. To give an example Lloyds Bank has shareholder value as the central objective of its mission statement. A firm may enhance its profitability by taking greater risks. It is thus important that any business be aware of the risks which it is taking and should not take risks inadvertently or without realising their magnitude. A key objective of an organisation may thus relate to the level of risk which it is prepared to undertake. There are no riskless businesses but some are more risky than others and it is a key commercial question as to the level of risk which the firm wishes to take. Enterprises in general wish to abide by the law and this may be a central issue particularly for those which are subject to detailed regulation, most notably the utilities and financial institutions. Where this is central to the operations of the firm then it should be a central issue in establishing management information systems.

STRATEGY

The management information systems that a firm establishes should be embedded in the strategy of that organisation. It is easy to see the techniques outlined in this book as being dedicated to enhance the trend towards centralisation within organisations generally in the western world. The improvements in management information allow the top management better to understand and control what is happening within their organisations. Although one can see this happening within many organisations it depends on the strategy of that particular organisation and these techniques are quite consistent with a devolved management structure. The strategy of an organisation can be seen as a specific set of proposals which will lead directly to the practical policies to achieve the goals of the organisation. In the formulation of strategy it is necessary to understand the external environment of the organisation and its internal capabilities. Then one must decide how, given these constraints, the organisation can best fulfil its objectives. Strategy must in essence be practical and its translation into plans, budgets and operational decisions must be transparent. The finance function within most organisations is central to the strategy formulation process since it will provide much of the basic information collection. It will also evaluate the financial implications of different strategic alternatives. Both balanced scorecards and activity-based management are vital to the strategy formulation and implementation process. In particular the development of balanced scorecards for an organisation will enable it better to establish meaningful and implementable strategy.

IMPLEMENTATION

Having established the strategy of an organisation it is then necessary to implement it. The standard tool in large organisations is to incorporate the strategy within the planning and budgetary process which is used to create targets for individual managers within the organisation. The implementation of strategy involves all major decisions and the activity of all individuals within the organisation being related to the strategy. This will be related to organisational culture, communications, and formal targeting, monitoring and motivational systems.

THE ENVIRONMENT

When the management of an organisation seek to implement their policy or strategy they will be faced by two sets of reactions which are subject to some degree of uncertainty. There will be the reactions within their own organisations, for example it is difficult to enter into a cost cutting programme within an enterprise without paying some price in terms of organisational morale. The understanding of the way in which an organisation will react to any policy changes is an essential part of the formulation of effective strategy. There is that wonderful term to describe the reaction of an organisation and its individuals to a policy of which they do not approve, malicious compliance. The reaction internally to policy changes in general are more easy to predict and have less important impacts than those which stem from changes in the external environment of the firm. The developments in the competitive process as, for example, a new effective competitor or a change in technology can have a much more radical impact. The archetypal example of this is what happened to the Swiss watch-making trade with the development of battery-based technology. In implementing strategy it is important to think of the different policy levers open to management and the degree to which their impacts can be predicted. Let us consider two examples; changing the price of a product and implementing a training programme to make staff more customer focused. In the first instance the firm can have extensive knowledge of the likely impacts of a price change on one of its products, since this will be a policy change which is frequently implemented and in all likelihood it will have attempted to quantify the impacts of past changes. The impacts of price changes can be predicted with some degree of accuracy. In contrast the implementation of a customer care programme is a much less frequent policy change for an organisation and its impacts are much more difficult to measure and certainly more difficult to turn into some quantification of the financial impacts of the policy. These examples just illustrate that the more radical the set of changes envisaged the greater the degree of uncertainty in predicting their likely results; combined with the insight that most life-threatening problems for an organisation are external. The internal and external environment to the enterprise thus create uncertainties in relation to the implementation of strategy which have central impact on the performance of the organisation.

RESULTS

The results will be the central outcomes for the organisation. They will depend on an interaction of the policy and the environment both external and internal to the enterprise. Given the levels of uncertainty there will be many feedback loops between strategy, implementation and results. The whole process, if it is to be successful, will involve reacting to new and unexpected circumstances.

In a sense this chapter has been an attempt to produce a logical overview of a co-ordinated management process, in most organisations it is much more chaotic. However the key to management information, and in particular the techniques which this book focuses on, is to put in place structures which make management and operations a more rational, controlled and better thought-out process. The use of the balanced business scorecard will aid in identifying objectives, creating implementable policy and ensuring that the organisation can implement its strategy. Activity-based management ensures that management action is focused on obtaining the required financial outcomes. The use of both techniques will improve the management of any organisation.

Part 2

Balanced scorecards

3

Introducing balanced scorecards

INTRODUCTION

The concept of a balanced scorecard was first introduced in the Harvard Business Review of January–February 1992 by Robert S. Kaplan, Arthur Lowes Dickenson Professor of Accounting at the Harvard Business School and David P. Norton, President of Renaissance Solutions, a consulting firm based in Massachusetts. They have subsequently published a number of other papers developing the concept in the Harvard Business Reviews of September–October 1993 and that of January–February 1996. In 1996 they published a book called *The Balanced Scorecard* which is based on their experiences in developing scorecards. Since these publications there has been a proliferation of firms producing scorecards to be used in developing and implementing their strategies. The following list of businesses is by no means comprehensive but does indicate the speed with which the technique is spreading through the business world. These are companies which have made some effort to introduce the concept to their management process:

- Apple Computers
- Mobile Oil Corp.
- Sears Roebuck & Co.
- Hewlett-Packard Co.
- Rockwell International Co.
- Rank Xerox
- Caterpillar Inc.
- Metropolitan Life Insurance Co.
- Anheuser-Bush Companies
- BellSouth Telecommunications
- New York University Medical Centre
- Analog Devices Inc.
- McNeil Customer Products Co.
- The Prudential Bank

- The National Westminster Bank Plc.
- The Abbey National Plc.
- Barclays Bank
- British Airways
- Halifax Building Society
- British Gas
- BP
- Skandia
- Nationwide Building Society.

This list gives some indication of the rate at which the concept has spread throughout the business community. There are many organisations which have developed scorecards but who are not prepared to attest to this in public forums. One major consultant has constructed some one hundred scorecards for separate organisations.

THE KEY USES FOR THE BALANCED BUSINESS SCORECARD

The concept of a balanced scorecard was developed as an antidote to a number of partial views of how a business should be managed. There have been a number of fashionable perspectives as to how enterprises should be managed, for example concentrating on short term financial indicators like profitability, return on capital; focusing on quality; some vital process or customer satisfaction. There are many different ways to manage a business, but the universal experience is that management seems to have far too many factors to concentrate on and it is easy to lose focus on what are the key factors. If it is easy for top management to lose focus then it is impossible to ensure that line management and staff see their activities as part of a co-ordinated management process. The balanced scorecard offers a number of advantages to an organisation that implements it. The key ones are:

- the ability to ensure that the strategy of the business is coherent and implementable

- the ability to ensure that the management information systems focus on the implementation of strategy
- the ability to communicate the strategy within the organisation
- the ability to ensure that the managers and their subordinates can see how their activities are related to the implementation of the strategy
- the ability to judge how well the organisation is progressing in terms of its strategy
- the ability to have an integrated management system for the organisation
- the ability to test how effective a particular strategy is for the organisation.

Just considering this list of objectives suggests that the technique will be of great use in the management of many different types of organisation. It is an excellent framework for strategy development and implementation, but it must be added that it is only as good as the strategy that an organisation develops. A poor strategy will lead to poor outcomes irrespective of what systems it is embedded in.

THE NATURE OF THE BALANCED BUSINESS SCORECARD

The essence of a balanced scorecard is to create a set of measurable indicators which reflect the key elements in the strategic process. The indicators relate to objectives, leading indicators of performance and necessary activities which must be achieved for the strategy to be successful. They are the objectives, leading and lagged indicators of the organisation's strategy. The attempt to articulate these will lead to a clearer specification of strategy and the way in which the organisation is expected to achieve its goals. The measures should be restricted in number so that they can be at the focus of management attention. The key to effective scorecards is that they are comprehensive and simple so it is possible to build an effective system for targeting, management and control. This can be developed for a whole organisation by cascading the main measures throughout the organisational structure.

The Kaplan and Norton articles divide the scorecard performance indicators into four categories which are the basis for four different sub-scorecards which make up the balanced scorecard. The four different sub-scorecards are as follows:

- The financial perspective – How do we look to shareholders?
- The customer perspective – How do customers see us?
- The internal perspective – What must we excel at?
- The innovation and learning perspective – Can we continue to improve and create value?

These perspectives are seen to be sufficient to reflect the most crucial elements of strategy formulation and implementation. Although, as we will argue, there is much merit in this fourfold categorisation, this structure should only be seen as a tool and if the strategy is better encapsulated in a scorecard with different elements then it is sensible to use another structure for that particular organisation.

The scorecard is seen as a way to move from the central vision of the company, be it to 'maximise shareholder value' or to be the 'premiere supplier of a particular type of service', to a coherent implementable policy. These visions, although all the individuals in the organisation may be aware of them, will not be sufficient to motivate the organisation in a coherent and unified direction. The four perspectives are seen to be central to the implementation of any strategy. If one considers the work of Richard Porter in the development of strategy, he focuses on the outside markets in which the firm competes and the internal processes which create value. The success indicators suggested by the scorecard may follow this type of Porter analysis. The generic strategies which can lead to success are to focus on an advantage in the way one produces the product sold or to focus on a particular market segment. These two approaches are easily accommodated within the structure of the standard scorecard.

THE FINANCIAL PERSPECTIVE

Over the past ten years there has been increasing financial pressures on all organisations in the developed world, be they corporates, mutuals, charities, local authority or governmental organisations. These pressures may take a number of different forms depending on the type of the organisation. If one considers corporates, then there has been increased pressure from the market to ensure adequate returns for shareholders. In particular there has been an increasing level of intervention in corporate affairs by institutional shareholders, two recent notable examples being in relation to British Gas and the role of Cederick Smith and the intervention on the remuneration package of the new managing director of GEC. This has led many companies in the United States and Great Britain to make shareholder value their key objective. To take two examples from the United Kingdom, Lloyds Bank and Abbey National Plc, both have mission statements related to maximising their shareholder value. However, if one considers the public and municipal sectors, there are increasing pressures related to the universal tightening of public expenditure constraints. Thus any organisation in establishing a scorecard should give focus to the financial elements in their plans and performance.

There are a number of different roles for financial indicators. They are frequently the key objectives of firms, be they in terms of profits targets or shareholder value. They are often the acid test of whether the strategy and its implementation is working. It is vital to understand in relation to the development of scorecards that it is possible to develop a coherent strategy for an organisation, and for that strategy to be embodied in a good scorecard, and for this to form the basis for the strategic information system of the organisation, but if the strategy is unsuccessful whatever the process the organisation will be a failure. Resources form the ultimate test for most organisations and if the strategy does not generate them then it must be changed. This book is focused on the correct process for the formulation of a world standard information system, it does not provide an infallible mechanism for generating successful organisational policy. It is very important to guard against the natural proliferation of management information and thus the scorecard indicators should have a central status above other performance indicators.

There has been much criticism of financial indicators in that they tend to be backward looking and fail to focus on the essential value creating features of the business, however they do have an objective quality which can most certainly be perceived internally in a business, and despite the many techniques for manipulating the published financial results, can also have an external validity. In the rituals of performance evaluation at least the key financial indicators have an extra company validity, which company specific indicators do not have. Whatever type of organisation one is considering there is value in having part of a comprehensive balanced scorecard devoted to financial indicators. Financial success enhances the resources available to any organisation.

One of the most interesting stories of the role of financial indicators in a scorecard is given in a White Paper by Renaissance Solutions on the World Wide Web which is also published in a 1996 issue of *Across the Board*. It cites a meeting of Mobile US' marketing and refining division, which contributes 80 per cent of Mobil Corporation's revenues, to discuss the first quarter 1995 results. The financial performance had been bad, due in part to the mild winter and the resulting low level of natural gas and heating oil sales. The senior management evaluation of the division's performance was unique in corporate experience, in that the focus was not on the results, but rather on the fact that all the factors which the division could control were behaving well. The staff expected to be heavily criticised but were in fact complimented. The framework within which this judgement was made was one of a balanced scorecard. One can debate the actual significance of the information in that it may constitute improved management and that results will follow directly from this approach or it may be that the strategy is misguided, it is too soon to tell. However, it does illustrate that the scorecard allows the focus on strategy implementation and allows a broader judgement than the pure financial. The financial perspective may be essential but the organisation has a future and the performance will be judged over time rather than in an individual time period, be it quarter or year.

The noteworthy aspect of this is the argument, particularly applied to the Anglo-Saxon world, that the short term financial performance of a corporate is the key focus of the capital markets. It is also observed that the capital markets in the Anglo-Saxon world provide a greater proportion of finance in comparison with, for example, Germany and Japan. Thus if a business focuses on the longer term and non-financial indicators it may be adversely judged. This has led Kaplan and Norton to speculate on the publication of key scorecard indicators. The argument may be that the scorecard is a technique for improving the focus of organisations particularly in the United States and the United Kingdom towards more strategic objectives.

To give some examples of the types of financial indicators to be seen in scorecards let us take the examples of Rockwater, a global underwater engineering and construction company and a company referred to as ECI both cited in the initial Kaplan and Norton Paper. The scorecards are illustrated in Figure 3.1.

Figure 3.1
FINANCIAL SCORECARDS

Rockwater	ECI
Return on capital	Cash flow
Cash flow	Quarterly sales growth and operating income by division
Project profitability	Increase in market share
Reliability of performance	Return on equity

Commenting on these indicators, there are certain expected similarities in the scorecards of the two companies. They are both interested in cash flow and profitability indicators. However, there are many differences which reflect the uniqueness of the two individual businesses. The cash flow indicators relate to the need for business, if it is to survive, to generate cash. This is a vital short term indicator of financial performance. Rockwell's key profits measure was in relation to projects whilst that of ECI was Divisional Operating Income. This reflects the types of business that the two companies were undertaking and what are seen to be the basic value creating units. Return on capital was considered by Rockwell whilst return on equity was the indicator for ECI. Rockwell is considering an indicator which reflects overall resource usage whilst ECI is considering only the return in relation to the shareholders' funds as valued in the balance sheet. Increasing market share was seen as a major indicator of future business performance by ECI. The last indicator used by Rockwell was reliability of performance. This was seen as a key indicator since the inability to forecast future performance was seen as a management problem in Rockwell.

That these indicators were specifically designed for the needs of the individual company can easily be seen, since they would not necessarily be the indicators that immediately spring to mind if one was asked to generate the key financial indicators. It is interesting to consider the financial issues which were not addressed by these indicators. Although cash flow was considered by both companies and return on equity by ECI these are not easily seen as being an exact indicator of the returns to the shareholder. Indicators like returns to shareholders, share price and market valuation of the company are more relevant indicators. It is also interesting to note that in Rockwater's scorecard there are no cost indicators. There is a single cost indicator in ECI's internal processes scorecard. It must thus be concluded that these were not seen as key strategic mechanisms for implementing and judging strategy for these businesses. Thus if one only considers financial indicators there is a great degree of flexibility as to which indicators should be chosen and it will depend on the strategic specifics of the organisation involved.

THE CUSTOMER PERSPECTIVE

It is vital for any business to satisfy the needs of its customers on terms which allow the business to achieve its objectives. If one considers organisations which are non-commercial businesses as, for example, charities or publicly funded organisations one can identify customers or their equivalent. If one takes, for example, the criminal courts, these have a number of customers in relation to people who are being tried for crimes, the state, lawyers, police, the probationary staff and so on. Thus any organisation or part of an organisation can have customers which are the individuals for whom it provides goods or services. Many company mission statements are expressed in terms of providing customer satisfaction. The scorecard must translate these into measurements which have specific significance in implementing any vision. There are two types of indicator which may be used, those which are related to issues which have significance for the customer and their behaviour and those which have significance for the organisation. If one were to consider those which have significance for the customer they might be in terms like time, quality, performance and service and price; this list was drawn up by Kaplan and Norton. A slightly different approach is taken in my book *Financial Management Information and Analysis for Retail Banks* in which the customer-based scorecard is based more on measures which have significance for the organisation. In essence the customer perspective should focus on those customers and customer segments that are considered vital to the goals of the organisation. This is illustrated in Figure 3.2.

These indicators are wider than those in the initial scorecards since they have general indicators of the customer performance of the company and the customer perception of the quality of the products. In using and interpreting these types of measure it may be necessary to survey continually the attitudes of customers of one's own organisation and one's competitors. Taking one particular example in the financial sector, the standard customer profitability profile for any retail bank is depicted in Figure 3.3.

Figure 3.2
CUSTOMER-BASED SCORECARD FOR RETAIL BANK

Customer attitude to the organisation

Profitability of customer groups

Sales by customer groups

Retention rates by customer groups

Image of company

Customer perception of product quality

Figure 3.3
CUMULATIVE CUSTOMER PROFITABILITY

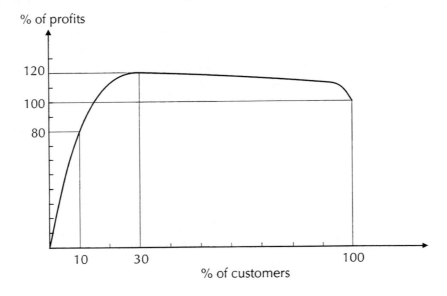

The 80/20 rule or Pareto rule when applied to the profitability of customers would appear to suggest that 80 per cent of a bank's profits will be generated by 20 per cent of its customers. In my experience of retail banks a 80/10 rule would be more appropriate. Other consultants have expressed differing views based on differing experience, for example, Alberic Braas has suggested a 220/20 rule.

The bank is thus very interested in the profitability and potential profitability of particular customer groups and whether it is managing to retain those key groups. This may be a key to its long term financial performance. Again one must stress that the nature of the scorecard which is generated may depend on the nature of the organisation one is considering and the specific strategy of that organisation. This picture for banking may be dramatic, but the usual outcome of any activity-based costing study applied to any business is to produce a profit diagram with the hook depicted in Figure 3.3. One cannot generate these specific scorecard measures without an activity-based costing system.

THE INTERNAL BUSINESS PERSPECTIVE

The internal business perspective focuses on those aspects of a firm's operations which provide value for the customers and are key to the operational success of the business. They will be different with each operation. Figure 3.4. gives two examples of internal business scorecards which have been developed for Skandia and the National Westminster Bank's Information Technology Group. The data on Skandia comes from a presentation by Leif Edvinsson, Director of Intellectual Capital, Skandia AFS at an Ernst and Young sponsored conference on 'Exploring New Values and Measurements for the Knowledge Era' and the National Westminster Bank data from a presentation by Andrew Barnard Manager, Balanced Business Scorecard, on 'Translating Corporate Objectives into Departmental and Individual Performance Targets, Leading to Performance related Bonuses' presented to an IIR conference on 'Effective Performance Management' 22 September 1995 in London.

It is not unexpected to note that there is no overlap between the indicators used in the two operations, since they should relate to the internal operations of business which are entirely different. They should be determined as all scorecard indicators by what is central to the organisational strategy.

Figure 3.4
INTERNAL BUSINESS SCORECARDS

Skandia AFS	National Westminster IT
Unit expense rates	Service/delivery performance
Contact turnaround	Manpower productivity
Phone activity	Time to market
	Unit Costs
	Capacity utilisation

THE INNOVATION AND LEARNING SCORECARD

If there is a central problem for all organisations it is the changing nature of the environment in which they operate. If an organisation does not change to meet the changing circumstances it will die. The innovation and learning scorecard attempts to ensure that sufficient focus is on change and improvement within the organisation. This is the key perspective if one wishes to revolutionise a business over time. Taking two examples of companies which we have cited earlier in Skandia and Rockwater their innovation and learning scorecards are illustrated in Figure 3.5.

This is in many ways the most difficult of all the scorecards to develop since it relates to how the organisation is preparing itself for the future. The indicators are in very general terms in the two examples which we have cited. However it is important that an organisation has a strategy for the future and that measures implemented to achieve it are associated with the system of strategic management. This tends to be the most difficult area to develop scorecard measures, since it is often difficult to decide on an appropriate metric. One suggestion which stems from Beer, Eisenstat, and Biggadike's article, 'Developing an Organisation Capable of Strategy Implementation and Reformulation'

Figure 3.5
INNOVATION AND LEARNING SCORECARD

Rockwater	Skandia AFS
% revenue from new services	Number of new products per year
Rate of improvement index	% premiums from new sources
Staff attitude survey	Growth rate/industry growth rate
Number of employee suggestions	
Revenue per employee	

is than when an appropriate measure is not available then one should use words describing the activities in a particular time period rather than a measure, this will ensure that a focus remains even where the aspect of policy is difficult to measure.

OTHER SCORECARDS

The Kaplan and Norton scorecards are based on the structure of four related scorecards. There is no necessity for this to be the case though the Kaplan–Norton does focus on issues and indicators which are likely to prove vital to any organisation. The key to the technique is that it should be the mechanism by which an organisation's strategy has its practical implementation. There may be benefits to include other types of measure or scorecards. In the December 1994 edition of *CA Magazine of Canada* A Willis suggests two other focuses which may be vital to an organisation, those of the environment and human well-being. The suggestion being that these factors are vital to long-term competitive advantage. The consideration of an organisation's objectives may, particularly for a non-profit-making organisation, be the basis for an important sub-scorecard. The other perspective which has always recommended itself to me is to have a risk scorecard which will monitor the factors which are considered to create the greatest potential risk for the organisation. There is in operation no correct way of ordering the factors for a strategic management system. The issues relate to creating a good and potentially successful strategy for the organisation and then designing an information system which will best reflect that strategy.

CONCLUSIONS

This chapter has introduced the concept of the balanced scorecard. It is a mechanism which will assist in the formulation of strategy. Once the strategy is designed it will enable the organisation to better implement that strategy since it can be communicated to the whole of the organisation and be made central to the activities of all the organisation's staff. It is a key measurement tool and can form the basis for cascading scorecards for all the units within an organisation.

4

The practical issues in implementing scorecards

INTRODUCTION

This chapter sets up the processes by which an organisation might introduce a balanced scorecard to its operations. It also attempts to explore the main difficulties which may lead to the project not generating all the benefits of which it is capable. The chapter outlines the whole processes needed if one is to make scorecards the central management tool for the organisation. If one considers firms in the real world they may already have systems and processes with which they are satisfied so it is not necessary to implement all the aspects of the scorecard system. It is possible to pick and choose depending on individual organisational circumstances. If, for example, one is happy with the remuneration system one does not necessarily have to establish this on the basis of a scorecard even if the organisation has a wish to introduce scorecards.

The process which follows is designed for implementation by a large corporate, but the techniques can be applied to an organisation of any size. There is an equivalent for any of the processes outlined in this chapter for the small business or non-commercial organisation.

THE KEY TO EFFECTIVE CHANGE

It is very difficult to make any major changes within any organisation without having the ostentatious support of senior management. If there is one factor on which balanced scorecards will fail it is if they do not have top management support, not just in terms of some speeches and quotes. It is vital for this to become a key top management tool. In the National Westminster Bank Plc it was introduced by the Chief Executive. At the EFMD Banking Seminar in March 1996 at the Reform Club Derek Wanless, the Group Chief Executive of National Westminster Group Plc., argued that the scorecard was a key to their long term view of the business. There are, however, examples where managers have argued to the contrary notably, Joseph Spadaford, a Senior Vice President of First Chicago Trust Company of New York, cited in the *White Papers* mentioned in the previous chapter, who suggests that setting up scorecards can galvanise staff even without top management sponsorship. The difficulty with this is how it fits within the strategic vision of the firm. It may be sensible for managers within large organisations to develop their own scorecards if there is no general system, but this will only benefit, at best the performance of one unit within an organisation. Thus for the greatest benefits to be obtained from the development of a balanced scorecard it is necessary to have sponsorship, commitment and participation from management at the very top. If they do not use it as a strategic tool then it is unlikely that the time effort and skills of the organisation will be devoted to make it a success.

Implementing a system where the balanced scorecard is to become the key management tool within the organisation is a *very* political process. It will be key to developing strategy, it will be key to judging operations and it will be key to making judgements on the success or failure of individuals. The system and the management information it creates will be a central playing field for organisational politics. It is thus important to implement it in a fashion which is not naive in relation to the realities of organisational politics. The process suggested is such that one should try to make the implementation as professional as possible and allow influence to be exercised in an open and sensible framework.

A PILOT PROJECT

If one is establishing a comprehensive management system based on the concept of the balanced scorecard it is highly unlikely that any sensible management of a large corporate or other organisation will introduce it in one stage for the whole organisation. The success of the technique depends on the ability of an organisation to be able to develop the scorecard and to use it as a management tool. The Kaplan and Norton view is that it takes time for an organisation to decide as to whether it has an effective scorecard. Its introduction is part of the process of institutional learning. This particularly conditions their attitude towards using scorecards as the basis for remuneration systems, a topic which we shall consider in greater detail later in this chapter. The view that having a pilot project is useful for scorecard development is substantiated by Keith MacDonald in a number of articles that he has written for the *Building Society Briefing* which is published by Ernst and Young in the UK. He argues that as an initial exercise in the development of a scorecard it is useful to learn by having two initial projects; one in regards to a particular business unit and one in regards to a crucial business process. My own experience would validate this argument, for any organisation developing a scorecard which is unique to its particular operations needs some practice in regards to it own problems. It is interesting to note that the company which manages its operations most strongly in the UK on the basis of a set of cascading scorecards, National Westminster Plc, prototyped its scorecards in its home loans business. In my view there are very strong practical reasons for having a pilot project even if one is totally convinced that management by scorecard is right for your organisation. It is also highly likely that any organisation setting up a scorecard system would wish to benefit from the experiences of other organisations so they would wish to employ a consultancy input to their process. Irrespective of the experience of the consultants they do not know your business so they need to be managed to ensure that they are facilitators rather than producers of what could be a vital tool for your organisation. Thus one can see consultants and academics recommend that a pilot would be a valuable part of any implementation process.

SETTING UP A TEAM

The implementation of a balanced scorecard system will require the setting up of a team. The brief and authority of the team may prove crucial to its success. If the idea is to provide the central strategic tool for organisational management then it should be sanctioned by the board and be the responsibility of a prominent board member if not the chief executive. The implementation team should reflect all the areas within the organisation in terms of representation. There should certainly be individuals involved in relation to corporate planning and the finance function, but it is important that their influence should not be overwhelming. In any sensible project it is important to benefit from outside expertise so the employment of consultants will provide an important input of objectivity and outside ideas. The central decisions in developing the scorecard must be the responsibility of the top management in the different parts of the organisation so the role of the scorecard team is to facilitate and develop the scorecards. It should report back on a regular basis to the highest forums of the organisation.

UNDERSTANDING AND DEVELOPING THE STRATEGY

The key scorecard for any organisation is that for the top level. It is likely to be the scorecard from which any cascading structure of scorecards derives its validity. It should be the story of the organisation's strategy. Many organisations have mission statements or corporate visions but it is not always clear how these are to be achieved or implemented.

The initial exercise will be to interview the most senior people in the organisation. The interviews of the 10 to 12 most senior people in the organisation should be the initial stage of the project. The interviews should focus on identifying the goals of the organisation and how it is attempting to achieve those goals. These interviews are attempting to understand:

• What are the goals of the organisation?
• Are these goals consistent?
• What is the way in which those goals are to be achieved?
• Is the strategy for achieving goals realistic?

Having identified the views of the top management it will be useful to develop a document which specifies the goals and strategy of the business and to confirm these at a management workshop with the most senior management which has been involved in the process of interviews.

This is the basic strategy document from which the high level scorecard for the organisation is developed. The purpose of the senior management workshop is to establish:

- the goals of the organisation
- the vital constraints under which it operates
- the process by which it will achieve it goals and fulfil its constraints.

The scorecard will reflect measures which relate to these three factors and the additional set of factors which are leading indicators in relation to these factors. The setting up of the scorecard requires measurement of variables which reflect these three or measure them directly.

It is also important to set up at this stage what I have termed the 'scorecard test'. The virtue of the scorecard approach is to give a balanced view of strategy. At this initial workshop the scorecard structure should be proposed and given validity. One will start by initially reviewing the Kaplan–Norton structure of financial, customer, internal business perspective and the innovation and learning perspective. It is then asked if this is the balanced framework in which the activity of this organisation is best contained. As we have suggested there are a number of other perspectives which have been used including, human relations, environment and risk. The purpose of this exercise is to enable any prospective scorecards to be tested against this initial overall perspective. The test is to ensure the measures proposed form a unified whole which reflects the overall vision of strategy. What is later proposed may be an improvement but the test will prevent the scorecard for the whole organisation being side tracked and therefore limited.

CONSTRUCTING THE SCORECARD

Having established the views of top management in regards to its strategy one is looking for variables which will measure whether strategy is being successfully implemented or not. A set of workshops with management throughout the organisation will enable a set of measures to be developed and tested. This is by no means an easy task since the result of this process will be to generate a large number of measures of the different aspects of the strategy. The measures will also be partial in that some of the factors will lead to good clear measures whilst others may not be easily measurable or lead to measures which are not clearly related to the factor one actually wishes to measure.

The key guiding principles should be to seek to generate a balanced set of indicators, since if it is not balanced, when it is used to implement strategy the implementation will be unbalanced. One should use the decisions from the senior management workshop to ensure that the scorecard is tested against their initial view of the scorecard components. It may thus be necessary to use measures which are not exactly what is required but, in general, balance is more important than exactitude. There may be two reasons for this either, there is no measure which reflects the variables one wishes to measure, or it will take time to ensure that one can measure the relevant variable. An example of this process is given in Figure 4.1. which is taken from an article in Ernst and Young's *Building Society Briefing*.

The target measures are those factors or variables which the organisation wishes to use as elements in its scorecard. If they are not available then one may wish to settle for measures which are good surrogates. To take the example of staff satisfaction one may find it difficult to measure this directly since even where one surveys the satisfaction of staff directly there may be measurement problems. I have been involved in staff satisfaction surveys where even though the results were being processed by an independent company many of the staff were worried that adverse comments would be identified to them

Figure 4.1.
INITIAL AND DESIRED MEASURES

Initial	Target
Surrogate measures	*Actual measures*
Staff turnover	Staff satisfaction
Project spend *v.* budget	Systems implementation benefit
Input measures	*Output measures*
Training days	Staff skills
Sales interviews	Loans on file per interview

and it might affect their job security. Thus one may have to settle in the short or long term for indicators which do not exactly measure the desired factor. One common problem with performance measurement is that it is often easier to measure inputs rather than outputs. This may be for many reasons, the outputs may not be standard or there may not be an easy mechanism of their measurement. In one of the examples above, that of staff skills, they are certainly measurable in principle, but there may be a diversity of different skills in which one is interested and they may require direct measurement and monitoring which is often far from easy. Kaplan and Norton in their 1996 book on scorecards also divide scorecard variables into lead and lag indicators of performance and suggest that a balanced scorecard should have a mixture of both. Considering Figure 4.3 which is derived from their book, a *Customer Satisfaction Survey* will give an indication of how customers view Metro Bank, whilst customer retention indicators will result from customer's attitude to the bank which will depend on the measurements in the customer satisfaction survey. Even if an organisation's strategy remains constant over time it may develop its scorecard as it becomes able to generate and measure more meaningful variables.

WHAT IS A GOOD SCORECARD?

Rick Anderson of BP in his presentation, 'A Practical Application of the Business Scorecard to Align Business Goal and Performance', to the Business Intelligence Conference on Business Performance Measurement in April 1996 outlines a set of criterion for a successful non-financial measurement system. He argued that there were five attributes which the performance measurement system should have. It should be acceptable, suitable, feasible, effective and aligned. His definitions of the terms was; acceptable – they can be understood; suitable – they measure important things; feasible – they are easy to collect; effective – they concentrate on encouraging the right behaviour; and aligned – the non-financial measures must link to financial goals.

These are certainly all elements which form the basis for a good scorecard, however it is important to add some extra detail to this perception. We have concentrated so far on the overall scorecard for the organisation and will continue to do so in this section, however all the points that we are making can be applied to scorecards for individual aspects of an organisation. The key aspects of scorecards for me can be summarised in the following terms:

Embody strategy

The scorecard is in essence a mechanism for implementing the organisational strategy. Thus any quick consideration of the scorecard should lead to a very specific understanding of the strategy of the organisation or the unit considered. If this is not possible then the use of the scorecard will not enable a balanced implementation of the strategy. The scorecard must thus reflect all the important aspects of the strategy.

It should not be over financial

If one asks the question of a commercial organisation, 'Why does it make profits?' the answer, if it is to be informative is unlikely to be phrased in financial terms. This point can be enforced by asking the question, 'can one value a business in terms of the historic cost embodied in its balance sheet?' A consultancy business, for example makes profits due to such intangibles as: its reputation, the skills of its employees and the business relationships of its employees. A strategy for success must focus on business issues and not financials. Financials are usually, though not always, the measure of success or failure. If a scorecard is a mechanism for the implementation and clarification of strategy then it cannot focus entirely on the financial.

It must be implementable

One of the initial worries about scorecards has been that the proliferation of measures which are considered crucial will confuse management and lead to less clarity rather than more clarity in action. The standard scorecard will have some 25 measures which the managers will have to consider in their operations. There will always be pressure to increase the number of indicators in the scorecard but this pressure should be resisted by asking the question, 'can the managers be expected to manage on the basis of this aggregation of measures?' This perspective will, hopefully prove an antidote to the proliferation of measures. There certainly can be a problem of prioritising measures and this may lead to confusion. The problem can however be met by realising that a good strategy, which is at the basis of a good scorecard, will have within it a coherent balance. It is difficult to focus on 25 measures but if there is a unifying vision of strategy embodied in the scorecard it becomes easier for management to understand the nature of the actions which are required.

It must be the subject of a learning process

As an organisation develops, even where its basic strategy remains in place, it will change the detail of the strategy. The scorecard should be subject to periodic review to ensure that it reflects any changes in the strategy. As I will argue that the scorecard when it is implemented within the organisation should become an integral part of the planning and budgetary process it should be reviewed as par to the annual planning and budgetary cycle.

The balanced scorecard should be balanced

The virtue of the scorecard is that it should give a management tool which reflects the way in which the business seeks to be successful. This should be reflected in the scorecard. The 'balance test' is a key mechanism for ensuring the scorecard is a reflection of the way the business should be run.

Given most organisations are uneasy to reveal their organisational scorecards in public, since they contain a specific articulation of their strategy, let me take a case study from Kaplan and Norton's Book which is called Metro Bank to illustrate the nature of a good scorecard. Figures 4.2. and 4.3. are derived from that book.

The problems of Metro Bank are seen to be excessive reliance on a single deposit account and a cost structure which makes 80 per cent of its customers unprofitable. This customer profitability perspective is not particularly unusual for the retail banking sector. Faced with these problems the strategy of Metro Bank is developed in terms of a revenue growth and a productivity improvement. The growth of revenue is to be accompanied by a broadening of the sources of revenue from additional products and the selling of additional products to existing customers. The essence of productivity growth is seen to be the shifting of unprofitable customers to more efficient distribution channels with, in particular, the development of electronic banking. The linkage in the strategy is illustrated in Figure 4.2.

Figure 4.2
THE METRO BANK STRATEGY

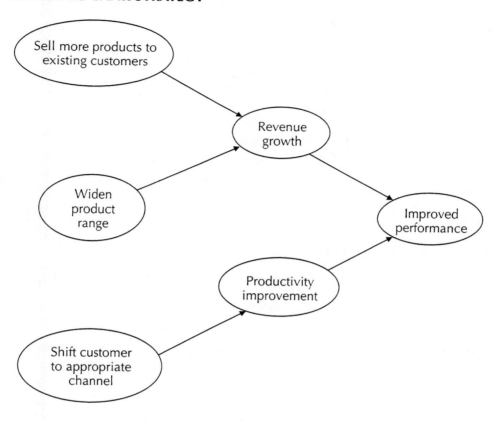

The strategy depicted in Figure 4.2. is organised from a scorecard perspective. It is initiated in the learning and growth perspective since the strategy is to radically change the operations of the enterprise. These changes will lead to a set of changes from the bank's internal perspective. Provided that these are successful, it will have an impact in improving the satisfaction of customers and their confidence in the expertise of the organisation. This will eventually be the mechanism to improve the financial results. The presentation of the strategy in this framework illustrates that the four-fold perspective is very useful for the depiction of strategy and this type of diagram is useful for the development of the scorecard.

Figure 4.3 takes the strategic objectives of Figure 4.2 and turns these into scorecard measures, some of which are lead indicators and some of which are lag indicators. This scorecard is the strategic scorecard for the whole bank.

Figure 4.3

Financial	Return on investment
	Revenue growth
	Deposit service cost charge
	Revenue mix
Customer	Share of segment
	Depth of relationship
	Customer retention
	Satisfaction survey
Internal	New product revenue
	Cross-sell ratio
	Channel mix change
	Product development cycle
	Hours with customers
	Service error rate
	Request fulfilment time
Learning	Employee satisfaction
	Revenue per employee
	Strategic job coverage ratio
	Strategic information availability ratio
	Personal goals alignment

Considering the Metro Bank scorecard it has the key requirements of a good scorecard. It is a clear and structured set of measures which transparently can be used to implement the bank's strategy. It focuses on the organisation's objectives and how they can be achieved. It is a simple dual vision of the bank's policy. It can be easily seen that, although there are 20 separate measures, the actions which they encourage form a single integrated set of actions. This is an example of a good scorecard.

COMMUNICATING THE SCORECARD TO THE ORGANISATION

If the managers and staff of an organisation have a committed understanding of its strategy then there is increased likelihood that it will be successfully implemented. In many organisations the strategy is such that it is difficult for staff to understand the exact role that they have in its implementation. The scorecard can become a key tool for the communication of strategy throughout the organisation and by using it as the key management tool they can understand the commitment of the organisation to the strategy. The process of developing the scorecard will involve the team drawn from different parts of the organisation and will involve top management. When it is finally developed it is important to have an official roll out programme for the organisation. It can be part of the process by which cascading scorecards for all the organisational units are developed. One of the perceived key uses for the scorecards is in providing a mechanism for ensuring commitment of an organisation to a particular goal. It has proved useful in change management programmes, assimilating firms which have been taken over and in joint ventures. It has the virtue of allowing the management of an organisation to ensure that all those within the organisation understand what their activities are attempting to generate.

CASCADING SCORECARDS

Although the scorecard was initially seen as a strategic management tool many organisations have seen the organisational scorecard as just the apex of a system of management information and control. To give some examples: Mobil US marketing and refining division generated its overall divisional scorecard in August 1994, it then asked the heads of its Strategic Business Units (SBUs) to design their own scorecards. There were some issues in relation to the consistency of the scorecards with the overall scorecard but the management wished to allow the SBUs independence in setting their scorecards so that they would feel ownership for the whole process. In the end a further 17 scorecards were generated which proved to be remarkably consistent with the overall scorecard. The system established was seen to be an important development since it was set up so that the scorecard elements could be monitored on an ongoing basis.

The National Westminster Bank Plc developed the balanced scorecard during 1994, it was applied to the planning cycle in 1995/6 and used to manage in earnest from January 1995. It has become the key management tool of the organisation and is cascaded down to sufficiently detailed organisational levels that it has become central to the setting of bonuses for individual workers. Taking the group IT function, a scorecard for the whole group was generated and this was the basis for the construction of 15 departmental scorecards. These departmental scorecards were cascaded down to form the basis for personal quantifiable objectives for 2600 staff.

The virtue of this type of system is that the strategy of the organisation and its method of implementation become central to the objectives and performance evaluation of individuals and organisational units. The process of establishing formal scorecards throughout the organisation is an effective method of getting the organisation to accept and understand the scorecard concept.

INTEGRATING THE SCORECARD WITH THE MANAGEMENT PROCESS

To embed the scorecard in the management process of an organisation will involve a number of major initiatives within the organisation. There are a number of key aspects which should be considered.

Information and systems

The essence of the scorecard is to establish a strategically driven management system. The indicators which become part of the scorecard may initially be ones which the management information systems currently hold, but these are unlikely to be the indicators which the organisation wishes to be the basis for the scorecard. It is highly likely that new indicators will have to be monitored. The regularity with which indicators are required will depend on the strategy and the level of the organisation which is focused upon. Figure 4.4. indicates the fact that the individual need for a particular piece of information may be different within the organisational hierarchy. The hierarchy of scorecards will require that top managers may only require to receive information on a longer time frame whilst supervisors on the line may wish to monitor the indicator on an on-going real time basis. There will certainly be a requirement for enhanced information systems as a result of the scorecard developments, both in terms of indicators for the scorecard and due to the scorecard's impact on creating a more implementable strategy which will additionally have information systems requirements. The scorecard can be the basis for the development of an information systems strategy, as is argued by David Withey Managing Director of Amelia Financial Systems. The cascading scorecards for the National Westminster Bank Plc have the figures in traffic light colours green for satisfactory, orange for borderline performance and red for unsatisfactory performance. Each unit gets its own printout on a monthly basis.

Figure 4.4
PERFORMANCE MEASURE

Recipient	Regularity
Chief Executive	Exception reporting
Executive Director	Quarterly
Departmental Manager	Monthly
Manager	Weekly
Supervisor	Real time

The planning and budgetary process

The planning and budgetary system are the key management tools within most organisations. If the balanced scorecard system is to be successful it must be set up to dovetail with these other management systems within the organisation. The easiest way to derive consistency is to integrate the planning and budgetary system with the scorecard. Figure 4.5 takes it inspiration from David Norton's presentation 'The Balanced Scorecard: Creating a Dynamic Strategic Management System' to the Business Process Management Conference organised by Business Intelligence in April 1996.

Figure 4.5
RELATING THE STRATEGY TO THE PLANNING AND BUDGETARY SYSTEM

STRATEGY	BALANCED SCORECARD	TARGETS	INITIATIVES

The strategy will lead to the development of the scorecard. It will, through the planning process, lead to a set of specific business initiatives being developed. This in turn will lead to the setting up of performance targets for the organisation which will be embodied in the balanced scorecard. Thus, as for every organisation unit one would expect a financial plan and a budget, there should also be a scorecard. Some of the overall plan and budgetary items will form part of the scorecard. The planning and budgetary system should be combined with the balanced business scorecard system and form one seamless whole.

Business decisions

In most large organisations there will be a standard system for making major decisions. In some cases, as usually for capital expenditure, it will involve a formal financial analysis and sign off process. Other decisions, as for example the launch of a new product, will also involve a decision making process which may or may not be formal. If one is to manage the company in a strategic manner then these decisions should be scrutinised for their fit with the overall strategy of the organisation. As part of their evaluation process the impact of each decision on scorecard variables should be estimated. If the scorecard variables are considered this will ensure that decisions are congruent with the organisational strategy.

Business initiatives

In any large business at any point in time there will be a proliferation of different initiatives taking place. To use a few of the popular titles of the past few years there will be TQM, benchmarking and process engineering initiatives. There are, I suspect, important human motives for these projects in addition to any merits that they individually might possess. If one is to be noticed within an organisation one must be seen to make an impact, if one is not to be bored then one must do something different. Often the staff which are subject to these initiatives find it difficult to see them within their organisational context and with the establishment of a scorecard one can better see their worth. In response to the use of the scorecard for remuneration one may see managers sacrificing performance in relation to one measure to enhance overall measured performance. The measures should form a logical whole and one way of ensuring this is to establish a hurdle level of performance for each indicator.

Remuneration

Given the power of a scorecard and its ability to create strategic congruence within an organisation, it is not surprising that some businesses should wish to use the scorecard as a basis for a system of performance related payments. Kaplan and Norton have been cautious in their arguments relating scorecards to pay. They have argued that the strategy of an organisation is a hypothesis and the scorecard's value depends on whether the hypothesis is sensible. A bad scorecard with a remuneration system tied to it will enforce bad strategy. If one is going to base pay on scorecard performance they argue the scorecard should be bedded into the organisation first. There have been a number of organisations which have based their remuneration on scorecards, but the first problem which they have faced is to ensure that the different indicators are given an appropriate balance. There has been a tendency to give a large emphasis or weighting to the financial indicators. This is also a reaction to the issue of how good is the scorecard, if one is unsure that the strategy will deliver the required organisational financial performance then one will only switch slowly to the non-financial measures. The National Westminster system introduced at the start of 1995 had some interesting aspects, in that it related financial bonuses to a number of different scorecard based performances. In the National Westminster Group Information Technology the bonuses were a combination of the group IT bonus, the departmental bonus and the personal bonus.

Thus the balanced business scorecard can be seen as the tool to integrate the operations of the business and give them a strategic focus. The degree to which the tool is used should depend on the confidence that the management have in the tool and the underlying strategy.

WHAT CAN GO WRONG?

If you consider what the scorecard attempts to do one can easily realise that it can have a major impact on the activity of individuals within an organisation. Although it can be used as a tool for allowing greater decentralisation it is in general unlikely to be used in that manner. It will invariably lead to greater centralisation. There is therefore a need for the strategy to be correct for the organisation. If it is not sensible then the technique for ensuring that the strategy is more rigorously implemented will lead to problems for the organisation. The more lax the implementation the more easily the organisation will avoid problems.

The concept of a balanced scorecard will cause some problems within commercial organisations where they have been in the past motivated by considerations of profitability or shareholder value. It will be a move away from financial to strategic control. There is evidence that some companies have been uncomfortable with this and based their remuneration heavily on the financial aspects of the scorecard. It may often be the case that companies which focus on non-financial goals as a means to be financially successful will have poor results. It is therefore imperative that in setting up a scorecard the mechanism by which strategy obtains acceptable financial results is very explicitly considered.

There are degrees of partial implementation which can be undertaken so that the scorecard does not play as vital a role for an organisation as is suggested in this chapter. It might be used as a strategic management tool for executive management only. It need not be the basis for the remuneration system. If it is only used in this partial sense it will have less organisational credibility than if it is used for all the tasks of which it is capable. If it does not have the backing of the top management it will not be used neutrally throughout the organisation.

Large organisations are of their very nature political, and if a scorecard is used as a basic tool for management and evaluation it will not be seen as a neutral system by individual managers. There will be a number of different ways in which they may try to subvert it. They will argue that the scorecards do not adequately understand their particular unit and may try to produce their own management information to show how well they are doing. To use the system is an ongoing fight to ensure its relevance and that management are committed to it.

Often in firms strategy changes regularly and this is not reflected in the management and information systems. It is important that any major changes in strategy are reflected in the scorecard. Once the system has been established running it in tandem with the planning and budgetary system will help to ensure its continued relevance. The whole set of scorecards for the organisation should be reviewed as part of each planning cycle to ensure that they are consistent with the current strategy. If there are major changes in the strategy they should immediately be reflected in the scorecards. It is thus very important to ensure that the scorecards have a system of regular and automatic review. If they become outdated they will be circumvented as a management tool.

The key issues in ensuring that scorecards are worthwhile for the organisation are ensuring that the strategy is good for the organisation, implementing it in a credible way with top management sponsorship and ensuring that it reflects any subsequent changes in policy.

CONCLUSIONS

This chapter has reflected on the ways in which a balanced business scorecard can be introduced into an organisation. It is a method which will aid in the development of a practical implementable strategy and the communication of that strategic vision and can be a central management tool in the implementation of that strategy. It is technique and is not a substitute for thought and imagination in the strategic and management process. If the strategic thought and execution is poor the quality of the management system based on it will not lead an organisation to success. It is however an excellent tool if used to back up an excellent strategy.

Part 3

Activity-based management

5

An introduction to activity-based costing and management

INTRODUCTION

The technique called activity-based costing was introduced by Robert Kaplan, Robin Cooper and Thomas Johnson in the late 1980s. It was an attempt to deal with a set of problems in understanding how the cost structure of an organisation is related to the business of that organisation. The ideas were advertised in contrast to the simple accounting techniques of cost allocation which the authors saw as the then current orthodoxy. The ideas embodied in activity-based costing were however used widely in many organisations to better understand their activities. In my experience of the banking industry most large UK organisations were using something similar before the great Harvard innovation. In fact I remember my surprise when I was first introduced to the technique, since it had been an approach, which in essence, I had already helped introduce in a major retail bank. However the technique and its developments have systematised these ideas and there has been a broadening of the uses of the techniques to give a wide range of benefits.

THE REASONS FOR THE INTRODUCTION OF ACTIVITY-BASED MANAGEMENT

The introduction of activity-based costing was justified in terms of its improvement on the standard allocation of costs associated with product costing. The traditional allocation process can be summarised as considering materials and direct labour costs which can be directly related to a product and then to apportion all other overheads on the basis of some simple allocation driver, as labour hours or machine costs, the selling costs also might be allocated on the basis of the number of sales to enhance the sophistication. The process can be illustrated, as it is in Figure 5.1. In considering the profitability of a product, the head office costs would be allocated to production support departments and then these costs, with their associated support costs, would be allocated to the cost centres directly involved

Figure 5.1
TRADITIONAL COST ALLOCATION TECHNIQUES FOR PRODUCTS

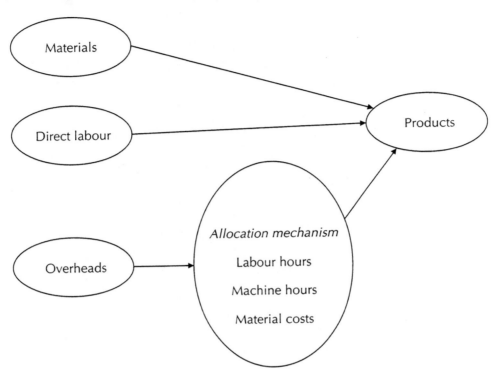

in production. The costs thus associated with the production departments would then be allocated to the products on the basis of labour hours, material costs or machine hours. These methods for relating costs to products are obviously simplistic. They were always a method of approximation. However as a method of approximation their accuracy has declined over the years with the increasing importance of technology relative to materials and labour as the basic determinant of the cost structure of most organisations. Robin Bellis-Jones and Nick Develin in their pamphlet for the Institute of Chartered Accountants of England and Wales cite an estimate that 7 per cent of total costs are direct labour whilst manufacturing overheads amount to 25 per cent of sales revenue. The benefits of a more subtle understanding of the cost structure appear to have increased as a result of the increasing importance of technology.

Bellis-Jones and Develin cite what is an apocryphal case study of a British engineering company which imported a complementary product from the Far East and which it sold from stock with little modification. The company absorbed its overhead costs on a direct labour basis and since the imported product required no direct labour it was allocated no overheads. The imported product did have an impact on a number of costs relating to purchasing, sales, invoicing, advertising, materials handling and distribution. The relative profitability of the imported product was seen as superior to the made to order products of the company, this comparison was based on a naive allocation of overhead costs. Although the example is simple, it illustrates that traditional cost allocation systems may mislead organisations as to the financial impact of their operations. If one considers operations where there are a large number of products as for example a retailing chain which may have 25 000 products the errors of this nature may have a major impact on the likelihood of the policy of an organisation leading to success and are less easy to detect. The general conclusion of most studies of activity-based costing in relation to more traditional allocation mechanisms is that usually too many costs were allocated to mass produced products and too little to products with short production runs. Activity-based costing will focus attention on costs like the diversity of products produced, the costs of setting up production runs and the costs of quality which are badly dealt with by traditional costing systems. In general this will emphasise the impacts cost on products with relatively low levels of output.

The essential motivation for activity-based costing and management is to better understand the way in which the cost and revenue structure of an organisation are influenced and so to manage those costs and revenues more effectively. Although the initial justification of its introduction was related to product profitability measurement, this is just, as we will see in the chapters that follow, one of the possible uses of activity-based costing information. Activity-based costing increases the subtlety with which costs are understood.

THE THEORY OF ACTIVITY-BASED COSTING

The theory of activity-based costing is entirely simple. It suggests that
the justification for costs is in the undertaking of activities which are
seen as necessary to the success of the organisation. The first step is to
draw up a list of activities in the organisational unit which is being
focused on. The nature of the activity list should depend on the uses to
which the analysis is to be put. The level of detail may vary from as
short a list of activities as 30 or, in my experience, the most being
4000. An example of the types of activity one may see, for example, in
a finance department is illustrated in Figure 5.2.

Figure 5.2
**AN ANALYSIS OF DIFFERENT LEVELS OF DETAIL IN THE DEFINITION OF
ACTIVITIES**

Aggregate level	Detailed level for the production of management accounts
Producing the financial accounts	Establishing forecasts
Producing the management accounts	Establishing budget parameters
Financial analysis	Iterations of budgetary submissions
Capital appraisal	Constructing budget
Payment processing	Budgetary sign off and communication process
	Monthly variance analysis and re-forecasting

The aggregate level activities would give a more general activity
picture of the Finance Department, whilst the more detailed level is to
take one item on the aggregate list, producing the management
accounts and to break it up into a set of more detailed activities. The

level of detail should depend on the uses to which the information is to be put. This point will be discussed in more detail in the sections on the implementation and the problems which may be faced by implementation. Having established the list of activities for the organisational unit one is considering, one should then go through a process of allocating costs to those activities. The activity-based costing exercise will be related to some cost base period. This might be the current budgetary period, last year's actuals, or the current re-forecast. The costs from some base information are allocated to the activity list. This should involve a specific analysis of each unit in the organisation. There are many ways in which this might be undertaken ranging from surveys and workshops to sophisticated operational research techniques. The costs of the organisation are thus divided so that they are related to all the activities on the activity list, these form what are frequently referred to as cost pools for the activities. The next stage is to decide on the factors which determine the levels of the activities these are called the activity drivers. Considering the aggregate activities of Figure 5.2 the activity drivers which can be associated with them are depicted in Figure 5.3.

Figure 5.3
EXAMPLES OF ACTIVITY DRIVERS

Aggregate level	Activity drivers
Producing the financial accounts	Legal Requirement
Producing the management accounts	Management requirement
Financial analysis	Number of decisions requiring analysis
Capital appraisal	Number of capital proposals
Payments processing	Number of invoices received

The activity drivers can usually be quantified, even those relating to the legal and management requirements since they imply one round of financial and management accounting each year. If one divides the expenditure on a particular activity by the number of units of its activity driver one obtains the activity rate, or the average expenditure for each unit of the activity driver. These activity rates allow the allocation of costs to different organisational perspectives, called cost objects which is at the heart of activity-based costing and management. There are many different ways in which the information can now be presented. It is however necessary at this point to introduce the revenues of the organisation and to relate them to the different organisational perspectives. Once this is undertaken one can give a financial focus to a diversity of organisational perspectives outlined in Figure 5.4. The information will allow the organisation to establish the profitability of its products, customers, distributional channel units, organisational units, business units, processes, decisions and can be used as a technique to classify costs which will be useful in implementation of any cost control programme.

Figure 5.4
THE DIFFERENT ALLOCATIONS OF ACTIVITY-BASED COSTING INFORMATION

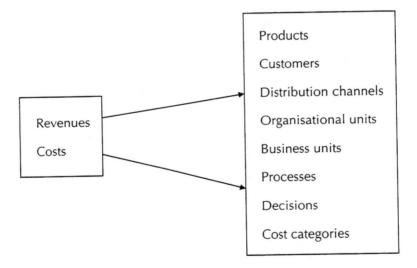

THE USES OF ACTIVITY-BASED COSTING

The uses of activity-based costing information are usually understood under the title of activity-based management. Activity-based management is the using of activity-based costing information in the management of an organisation. The key to improved management is depicted in Figure 5.5. In most organisations it is easy to track how its revenues are generated, it is much more difficult to understand exactly why costs are incurred. Activity-based costing allows the more effective understanding of the processes which generate costs. One of the essences of sensible management is to understand the relationships between costs and revenues. Activity-based costing spells out the nature of that relationship. This is a key to activity-based management. Considering each of the component parts of activity-based management:

Figure 5.5
THE GENERATION OF COSTS AND REVENUES

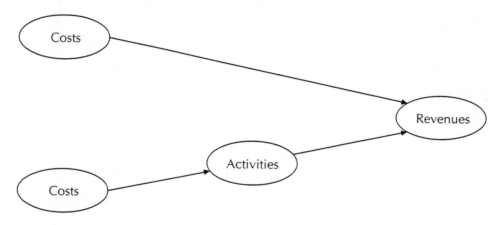

Strategic management

The strategy of a business does not directly follow from an understanding of its cost structure. Neither does it stem from any financial analysis based on that type of information. However to effectively formulate strategy it is essential to understand the financial profile of the business. Where one is trying to formulate a future strategic path it is vital to submit it to a financial scrutiny. The main reason for the scrutiny is not that one will take the numbers generated with any great deal of seriousness but that they are an intellectual discipline which will ensure that strategy is the subject of detailed thought. The use of simulation models will be one means of understanding the nature and risk of different strategic paths. The information derived from an activity-based costing exercise will form the basis for understanding the development of costs as part of different strategic visions. One of the interesting comparisons between Japanese and Anglo-Saxon management accounting has been the targeting of costs in product development. The manipulations which are made to activity rates as part of the strategic process can incorporate any targets for the organisational cost structure.

Product profitability

The initial arguments in relation to activity-based costing related to the development of sensible product profitability information. The introduction of activity-based costing will enable a commercial organisation to better understand the financial impacts of its product offerings. In conjunction with the other types of information generated, as for example, in relation to customers and distribution channels, it can provide vital information in the development of marketing policy. Product profitability information can be used to determine whether the products offered are financially viable and whether they should be offered to the customer. It may also be a central input into the pricing decision. Although it is important to base prices on many other facets than just the cost structure, an understanding of cost is an essential element in any sensible pricing decision. The production of regular product profitability data is important as a scanning tool to see if there are any profitability problems in relation to the firm's product line, this is especially useful where the range of products offered is very large. Having identified problems then a specific investigation as to what is the sensible policy response should follow. The understanding of the cost structure obtained by an activity-based costing exercise will form a useful input to any analysis of specific policy response to product profitability problems.

Customer profitability

Activity-based costing information allows the establishing of the profitability of each and every customer of an organisation. This will usually reveal that some of the customers, and often some of the best customers of an organisation, do not generate profits. We have referred to this in previous chapters in relation to the banking industry, but these results span every different type of commercial venture. The fact that a customer is not profitable is not, of itself, a reason for ending that relationship. There may be a series of different reasons why one might retain unprofitable customers, these are depicted in Figure 5.6.

Figure 5.6
SENSIBLE REASONS FOR RETAINING UNPROFITABLE CUSTOMERS

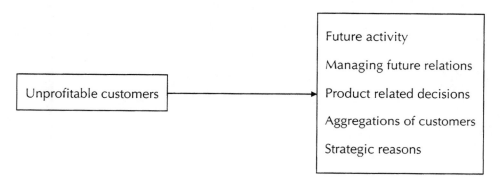

There will be customers who are currently unprofitable but who are developing their relationship with the organisation in question and that relationship will be expected to be profitable in future. These customers should be retained. If an organisation introduces an activity-based costing measurement of customer profitability there will be customers with which the organisation will need to change their relationship. This may require a renegotiation of the customer relationship so that they become profitable and in some cases it may involve terminating the customer relationship. When one considers the organisational strategy there may be products which are offered on an unprofitable basis, these may imply that certain customers are unprofitable and that one is prepared to live with this situation. There are often relationships between an organisations and groups of customers and it is sensible to see them in aggregate. Where members of a family are customers how one treats one may have an impact on all the relationships, in this situation a family rather than a customer policy may be appropriate. Coutts bank which is now a subsidiary of the National Westminster Bank Plc has a customer database which includes the relationships between its customers and they form a basis for some policy decisions. There may be strategic reasons for tolerating unprofitable customers, for example as part of a strategic attempt to improve one's competitive position.

Distribution channels

Measuring the relative profitability of different distribution channels and units which compose them has always caused some problems for commercial enterprises. The fact that Marks and Spencer only decided to institute this type of system in the last few years indicates that it is not entirely clear what messages one can derive from understanding the cost and revenue information of different units in distribution channels. However in most retailing enterprises the costs and revenues generated by distributional units are a major financial impact for any organisation so this information although often difficult to interpret is useful for any management of the organisation's distribution channels.

Organisational and business units

Activity-based costing associates the costs and revenues of organisational and business units to the activities which they undertake. It can give an understanding of the impacts on costs and revenues of different types of policy. This may lead to an improvement in the management processes within an organisation.

Processes

Recent years have seen a vogue in the United States and the United Kingdom for process engineering. Much has been made of the reservations expressed by its initially most active proponents in order to denigrate the impacts of the technique. It is based on a simple set of insights. Processes invariably span organisational units in different chains of command in the businesses structure. Where they span these units there will tend to be a lack of sensible co-ordination. Processes are also often in organisational units responsible for elements in a number of different processes, this may add to the problems of efficiently organising processes. A review from the process perspective will invariably, in such circumstances, reveal inefficiencies. If one adds to this new perspective the idea of introducing new information technology it is not surprising that this may lead to major improvements in quality and efficiency. Where these improvements lead to redundancies or increasing the intensity of the work process they are likely to cause problems of morale. The isolation of processes from an activity-based costing perspective will enable an understanding of the cost structure of the organisation and may prove a prerequisite for improving efficiency.

Decision support

The information obtained from an activity-based costing exercise can be used to support financial analysis of decisions, as for example, capital expenditure decisions. It becomes a vital data base for the organisation.

Cost control

The topic of cost control has been part of a number of the issues considered above, it is part of the strategic issues, it is integral to the section on process management, but one needs to consider it as a separate reason for introducing activity-based management to an organisation. There are a number of different ways in which an activity-based costing exercise can form the basis for cost control within an organisation. They are using it as a basis for: specifying strategic cost levels; influencing customers to have a lower cost relationship with the organisation; undertaking a cost review exercise; supporting process engineering; and the establishing of a system of activity-based budgeting. Considering each of these in turn:

An activity-based costing exercise will establish cost levels for the activities and process within an organisation. These will be unit costs. Having identified these cost levels they can be considered as part of the strategic planning process and their improvement seen as an important strategic goal for the organisation.

The way a customer conducts its business with an organisation often determines the costs of that relationship. If one can influence customers it may improve the financial position of the organisation. The drive by public utilities to have their customers pay by direct debits has provided many financial advantages, notably the lower costs of electronic means of payment, lower bad debt and improved cash flows. Activity-based costing can provide an organisation with the detailed information that allows it to understand which customer behaviour patterns are best for that organisation.

There are a number of different ways to conduct a cost review exercise in conjunction with activity-based management. As part of the cost collection exercise one can classify costs. The two most common classification systems are outlined in Figure 5.7. Considering those titled A, core activities and their resulting costs would be seen as those which directly add value, as for example selling, whilst support activities would be those which are necessary to enable the core activities to be undertaken, for example order handling, diversionary activities would be those which are created by some deficiency in the organisation, as for example complaint handling. A cost review would focus on the elimination of costs related to diversionary activities, and enhance the efficiency of core and support activities. The classification titled B is an alternative method of considering activities and their resultant costs. Business sustaining costs are those which add value to the business' customers whilst supporting costs are those which are not customer related. These are cross classified into necessary and discretionary. A cost review in this context will consider whether discretionary activities should be undertaken and, if they should be undertaken, how they can be performed more efficiently, and how necessary activities can be undertaken more effectively. An example of discretionary business supporting costs would be those costs relating to the financial analysis of decisions. These costs can be seen as justifiable and being either discretionary or supporting does not imply the costs are incurred because the organisation is inefficient.

Figure 5.7
CATEGORIES FOR COST REVIEWS

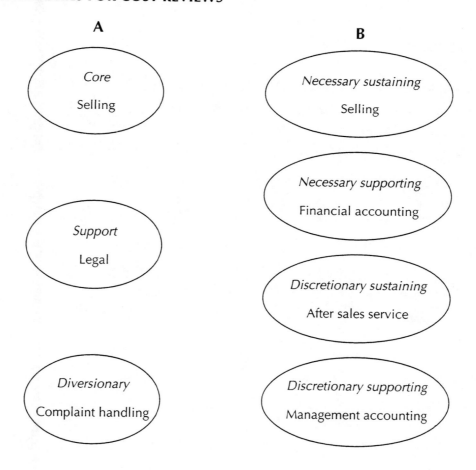

The establishing of a process engineering project and its monitoring will require some understanding of the resources applied to the process, so activity-based costing information can be helpful in lowering costs by this method.

The final mechanism for cost control is activity-based budgeting. That is the use of activity-based costing information to establish the standard costs of the organisation and use these as the basis for the setting up of the budget and the variance analysis applied to the actual outcomes.

The essential feature of activity-based costing is to better understand an organisation's cost structure and thus it is not surprising that one of its key purposes is to enhance the ability of an organisation to control the levels of its costs.

CONCLUSIONS

Activity-based costing is a technique by which an organisation can improve the understanding that it has of its cost structure. The technique has been introduced into many large organisations worldwide and will provide the organisation using it with an ability to change the process of its management by the introduction of activity-based management. The management will be provided with a very specific insight as to the implications of policy on the financial returns of the business. Thus it can be used to improve strategy formulation, customer policy, product development and marketing policy, the internal processes of the business and control over its operations and cost structure. It is a key tool for improving organisational management.

6

The practical implementation of activity-based management systems

INTRODUCTION

This chapter is based on my experience in managing and working on activity-based management systems in retail banking organisations. My particular experience is broadened by considering the experience of other professionals and the literature on the subject. Rather than consider a particular instance this chapter is expressed in terms of general principles. The next chapter deals with the specific pitfalls that one may encounter with the technique and its implementation, however the material in this chapter is designed as much as possible to set up an implementation project which will avoid those pitfalls. The chapter is a chronological description of the best way to implement an activity-based costing exercise and making it the basis for activity-based management within an organisation. The process thus described will be for a large organisation, it may however be applied on a smaller scale to organisations and businesses which are in the SME category. It can also be usefully applied to the public and not for profit sectors. There is no basic conflict between the implementation of activity-based management and the existence of a balanced scorecard within an organisation. Activity-based management focuses on the understanding of some of the financial implications of activity, a better understanding of which will direct policy to improve financial performance whilst the balanced scorecard offers a strategic context for the whole of a firm's operations.

THE ORGANISATIONAL GROUNDWORK

If one is to introduce any new management system this will have a major impact on how the organisation is managed and how individual's performance is measured. If this is to work it is essential to ensure that the project, as part of its brief, is trying to convince all those who are associated with it in the organisation that it will prove useful in improving organisational performance and that it will establish a more sensible and useful framework for the activities of individuals and in particular managers. As is said in numerous similar situations top management sponsorship is central to the success of any project. To obtain this is often easier said than done, since it is not that difficult in large organisations to get overall sponsorship, but what is required is to obtain support which is ongoing and seen to make this project among the key priorities of the top management. Top management support is needed if the project is to overcome any resistance to the introduction of any new management techniques. The introduction of a complete system of activity-based management will invariably meet with some resistance, particularly if it focuses on cost control or is the basis for a budgetary and performance measurement system. Part of the project should be to sell the virtues of the technique throughout the whole organisation. The greater the general conviction that these are sensible management techniques, the easier it is to introduce change through this type of project. In summary, top management must be convinced, the greater their participation the easier it will be to introduce change, but one must also focus on convincing line management of the merits of any new management or information system.

DECIDING THE SCOPE AND SETTING UP THE PROJECT

One of the most frequent pitfalls in establishing an activity-based costing system and the resultant activity-based management system is that the information base is not suitable for the purposes for which it is to be used. If policy and operational control systems are based on a poor information source then the results may be detrimental to the functioning of the organisation, will lack credibility and thus will not be fully implemented. The vital point is that the information collection exercise should be such as to provide information of the correct level of detail and focus in order to support the organisation's decision as to which of the many perspectives of activity-based management are to be implemented. The detail necessary to support a cost reduction programme will be greater, for example, than to support a general strategic review of the organisation's operations. If one is interested in modelling the impacts of the organisation's activities then it is necessary to understand how the costs of the organisation react to changes in the volumes of activity. There is much discretion as to the detail of information which can be collected and this will determine the degree to which one can sensibly implement the different aspects of activity-based management. Thus deciding the objectives and scope of the programme is vital and then ensuring that the detailed development of an activity-based costing system supports those decisions is the way to ensure an effective implementation of the technique. The important principle in deciding the level of detail is to ask which of the proposed uses requires the greatest level of detail and decide on the level of detail to satisfy that usage.

This key point should be reflected in any planning for the introduction of activity-based management to an organisation. The project will require an initial team to set up the project and they will be responsible for setting up the parameters of the implementation, producing a project plan, obtaining the precise consent and support of top management and then the setting up of the implementation team which will undertake the project. It may be sensible to have a pilot project to ensure the implementation team have sufficient experience to extend the implementation throughout the organisation. The issue of experience is important since the development of what may prove to be a central system of management, control and information should be created drawing on wide experience of this type of exercise. The training obtained by a pilot will prove invaluable for the future development of activity-based management. I would recommend that an organisation draws upon outside experience, if it has never engaged in this type of project, since it will be invaluable. The experience can be drawn either by employing individuals with this type of background in their previous jobs, or by the employment of consultants who will have diverse experience of these types of project. The setting up of a pilot project which is based on focusing on an organisational problem may prove particularly useful in getting activity-based management established within the organisation. Examples of the types of pilot project one might consider are to reduce costs within a particular operational unit, identify some loss-making products, or the consideration of particular customer group and how their profitability might be improved. If these can be isolated in a particular business unit, so much the better. This type of pilot will give confidence in the technique and can be seen to lead to immediately financially useful results. The initial pilot project should be designed not to cover the whole of the organisation since its purpose is a learning and propaganda exercise, so care should be taken to ensure a sensible and worthwhile issue is identified.

Thus there should be an initial team to set up the project by developing an overall plan for implementation of activity-based management in the organisation. The plan should scope the initial prototype scheme. It is best if this prototype focuses on an individual business unit since this can allow the many different perspectives of activity-based management to be explored. The plan should try to see the introduction of activity-based management as a modular system of implementation so that there is a degree of continuing choice for the organisation. However each phase should be conditioned so that it is not inconsistent with what follows. It can be a serious problem if activity-based management is implemented in a piecemeal manner where the earlier work has to be revisited to further develop the programme. Thus the programme should be drawn up in the awareness of the maximum impact that the project may have. In association with the development of the plan should be a financial analysis of its possible impacts in order to provide a benchmark for the value of the project's implementation. Having drawn up the plan and its financial justification the sign off should be obtained at the highest level in the organisation. This most sensibly should take the form of a decision to implement the project in a series of phases dependent of the perceived success of each stage. The culmination and evaluation of each stage to be considered by the organisation's executive to decide on the merits of moving to each further phase.

Having obtained overall support for the initial implementation the next phase relates to setting up the infrastructure of the project. The scheme should be the specific responsibility of a member of the executive team of the organisation so that they can be personally associated with the project, if this can be the chief executive then the project will be perceived to have extra organisational support and kudos. A management team for the project will also add weight to its importance, particularly if it is drawn from top management throughout the organisation. It will also help the project obtain resources and assistance from all the departments within the organisation. The work in developing activity-based management will require a team of workers to actually implement it. There are a number of possibilities for the membership of this team. It could be drawn, for example, from the finance and planning department staff. This may not, in fact, be the best choice of membership for the following reasons. The idea of activity-based management is to build a management system which will be used by the whole organisation and there may be doubt as to whether the finance staff adequately understand the operations of individual organisational units. The development of a multi-disciplinary team will enable specialist knowledge of the individual areas to be incorporated into the activity-based costing information, it will give all the main organisational areas some degree of responsibility for the project, it will lead to enhanced co-operation, since requests for co-operation can be made by individuals with a wider degree of organisational contacts and finally it will prove easier to sell within the organisation since the culture and approaches of the different departments will be reflected within the project's results. Although I would strongly recommend the establishing of a multi-disciplinary team from different parts of the organisation, there may be some problems in relation to skills, especially in relation to information technology and financial understanding, but these can be overcome by the selection of appropriate individuals and the setting up of sensible training to ensure that all members of the team have appropriate skills and understanding for the roles they are going to fulfil.

Therefore the project will require an initial team to scope the project, develop a project plan, provide a financial justification, obtain top management support, set up the organisational structure for implementation and bring together the implementation team. It is vital that the project plan ensures that the information gathering and the proposed nature of the implementation are consistent, since if they are not there will be many problems with the information base and the resulting implementation.

DEFINING THE OUTPUT

If one is applying activity-based costing to an organisational unit or, for that matter the whole organisation then it is vital to define in advance the precise nature of the informational output to be produced. To some extent this should be done in setting up the initial project plan, since this will identify the overall purposes of the project and how they will be achieved. The plan will identify the information which is to be used to create, for example, an information system, developing, customer and product profitability information; or whether the information is to be used as the basis for a cost control exercise. However this does not specify the output required at a detailed level. If, for example, one is constructing a product profitability information system, it will be necessary to specify all the products and the nature of the information formats to be produced. There is one point of key importance here, it is often the case that the output from an activity-based costing system is seen as a set of regular reports, this is in my view a very mistaken attitude. If one establishes regular product profitability reports, for example, the profitability of individual products is likely not to change over time and provided the range of products is limited the organisation may not need an elaborate system to tell it that which it can easily guess. However they may provide an early warning system for problems. Much of the key product profitability information is the result of using the base activity-based costing information for ad hoc analysis for policy support. The identifying of the correct information should not, therefore be confined to setting up of regular reporting systems, it should also consider the vital role of decision support analysis. The first task in setting up the project is to define the information which is to be produced so that both the information gathering process and the systems to be built to incorporate the information are fit for the purpose they are required for.

IDENTIFYING THE ACTIVITIES AND COLLECTING ACTIVITY-BASED INFORMATION

Having established the purposes for which the information will be used, the next task is to develop the activity list. The activity list is central to the quality of an activity-based costing exercise. It defines the level of detail which can be incorporated in any information which is produced. If a group is asked to define a set of activities which will comprehensively describe the totality of a business operation, this will present some difficulty. If members of the project team have been involved in the past on product costing, this may bias the definition of activities. It is important to draw up the activity list with a great degree of care. The broad principles which can be applied in deciding the activities which should be included are as follows. Firstly the activities should be such that the information gathered is sufficient for the objectives of the project. It should reflect the purpose which requires the most detailed organisational understanding. Secondly the activities should form a comprehensive picture of the organisation. All the organisational costs will have to be attributed to some activity or other. Thirdly the level of detail should be such that sensible information on the cost centres can be obtained. This will depend on the information gathering process. A general principle is that the greater the level of costs in a particular type of cost centre, and the greater the degree of complexity of those cost centres, the greater the degree of detail required in defining the activities of those cost centres. In a retailing organisation the selling outlets may comprise 50+ per cent plus of an organisation's costs and be composed in a number of different cost centres which undertake identical activities. Because of the importance of the financial impacts of these units it is worth spending considerable time and effort to understand the exact operations of these units. The activities should be defined for these in some degree of detail. Many other cost centres within an organisation, however, are unique and individually they are not responsible for a large proportion of the total costs. In these cost centres defining some ten to twelve activities at most is likely to be sufficient to define the operations of these units.

The project team should attempt to draw up a draft activity list, this can be undertaken provided the team is recruited from units throughout the organisation. Where a group of consultants is employed on the project and they have experience of this type of organisation, they should be able to provide a draft list of activities as a starting draft which can be modified within the project team. The draft list should be checked with all the cost centres involved. The mechanism for checking will depend on the way in which the costs are allocated to the activities. If one is relying on collecting information through a series of workshops then the checking of the activity list should be part of this process. The list will need to be accompanied by a definition of each activity in the list, this will be very important in ensuring data integrity. The activity list is unlikely to be entirely adequate and will be improved progressively throughout the information gathering process. It is important to use the expertise in individual departments to ensure the definition of activities is comprehensive and sensible. The deriving of an activity list is central to the whole exercise, so it is sensible to pay the price of some iterations in the information gathering process, for this will ensure the quality of the information and the benefits which the organisation can derive from that information. Definition and listing of the activities is vital to the success of any activity-based costing project.

ALLOCATING COSTS TO ACTIVITIES

The justification for any cost is that it is incurred in order to undertake an activity necessary to the organisation's operations. The allocation of costs to activities is a central building block of the activity-based costing project. It is in many ways the key information stage. There is a wide degree of discretion as to how this process can be undertaken and there are no set rules which can be followed. The individual solution will depend on the level of resources allocated to the project, the information which is already available to the organisation and decisions as to which cost centres should merit extra attention because of their complexity and importance.

Having determined the degree of detail in deciding the activity list one then has an idea as to the activities which will be undertaken in a particular organisational unit. The units should be classified in terms of five categories: whether they are unique units or whether there are a number of other units in the organisation which are identical; the level of resourcing that the unit requires; whether there is currently information in existence which can be used to help undertake this task; the estimated degree of complexity of their operations and to what extent their operations may be important for the overall nature of the project. The first two issues relate to the financial importance of the analysis of a particular unit and the latter three are related to their likelihood of causing problems in the project's analysis. A review of these issues will determine the level of resourcing devoted to an activity analysis of a particular type of cost centre. There is no requirement that one should treat cost centres in the same way since information gathering resources should be allocated according to the above priorities. There is a range of choices as to the techniques which can be used.

The initial implementation will require a decision as to what will be the base information to be used in the project. The cost structure will be investigated in relation to some budgetary based vision. The costs in relation to a particular period will be allocated to activities. The periods which may be used would include the budget for a particular time period, perhaps a year, the actuals and the re-forecasts during the current budgetary period. Thus actual costs for a particular year may provide the base period for the project. This cost information will be used to extrapolate information for other time periods as part of the application of activity-based costing.

INFORMATION COLLECTION

Having established the initial list of activities, the costing period for which the information will be collected and identified the way in which the information tying costs to activities is going to be gathered, one may initiate the information gathering process. The process is to fulfil the following objectives: to confirm the list of activities for the organisation; to understand the ways in which costs can be allocated to activities; and to understand what factors drive activities and the resultant costs. The form of the data collection will be dictated by the information that the project is to use and the way in which the data is to be modelled in terms of the precise systems to be used.

There are a diversity of ways in which the information can be collected. It is however likely that, whatever information gathering processes are used, a set of information gathering workshops will be employed. These workshops will serve a dual purpose, they are important for the information which they gather, but they are also an excellent opportunity to proselytise management as to the nature and benefits of activity-based management for the organisation. They will, if conducted correctly, give a degree of ownership of the information to their participants. As a general principle they are useful to consider unique cost centres within the organisation. These cost centres individually are unlikely to be responsible for a large proportion of the organisation's costs, but in aggregation may be responsible for up to 50 per cent of costs. The inviting of their managers to the workshops will provide an opportunity to convert a large proportion of the middle management to the merits of the project. Each workshop participant can be provided with the draft list of activities. They are to consider the list of activities and set them against the operations of their unit so that they can develop a list of activities which are undertaken in their unit. They are to be advised that the activity list is tentative but should be used as the basis for their departmental activity list. They are asked to highlight where they have identified new activities and where they have used an activity defined in a different way from the activity definitions which accompany the activity list. The workshops will take place over a period of time and the activity list will change over the course of the workshops. This will involve some iteration for workshop participants to change their submissions in relation to the evolution of the activity list. Having identified the precise nature of the list which applies to their cost centre the management should consider their resources in terms of different grades of manpower and operational costs and allocate them to activities on the list in terms of proportions or percentages. This will allocate costs to activities. The final task of the workshop is to suggest the factors which drive the levels of activity and therefore costs in the different units.

The information thus gathered will enable the activity list to be finalised, the distribution of costs to activities, and will provide a tentative insight into the factors which drive the costs in the units. The cost drivers identified are very important since they will give information on the degree to which costs are controllable in a particular cost centre. The cost driver list should be seen as tentative and a final list will be drawn up by modification when considering the uses to which the information is to be employed.

In tandem with the workshop programme any other data collection exercise should be undertaken. This may involve considering research which has already been undertaken in the organisation, again most organisations have undertaken some time and motion and statistical analysis of their main processing operations. This type of data may not be entirely suitable for the operation but in some cases provides crucial information. In cost centres which undertake complicated operations, and where there are a number of cost centres which consume a large proportion of the organisation's resources, it may be sensible to commission studies, be they statistical, survey or operational research, to understand activities and how they relate to costs.

When this collection exercise is complete the information will form a basic input to the analytical system used for the activity-based management. It is however not the complete set of information requirements which are necessary for the project. There are a number of other types of information which will need to be incorporated in any activity-based costing application. The precise requirements will depend on the objectives set for the project, but will probably include the following information; the information contained in the budgetary and planning system, by cost centre and aggregations of line items, a breakdown of the revenue in relation to products, customers and even activities and an identification of activity and activity driver volumes in relation to all the different cost objects of the project. The collection of these other items will require the use of existing systems and in some cases will depend on an extra collection project. The precise nature of the gathering of these other types of information will be organisational specific since it will depend on the choices in regards to how activity-based costing and management will be implemented and the current information systems of the organisation.

ACTIVITY-BASED SYSTEMS

The systems solution for an activity-based costing and management project is central to the development of an effective project. Although there are a number of proprietary activity-based costing systems on the market in the United Kingdom and overseas there remain three choices as to the nature of the system to be employed; one can buy and directly implement an 'off the shelf software package', one can buy a software package and customise it, or one can construct one's own system based on the peculiarities of the individual organisation. There is no unique choice as to the correct solution, but there are a number of considerations which should be borne in mind in relation to the choice, these are outlined in Figure 6.1. Discussing each of the factors individually:

Figure 6.1
FACTORS DETERMINING THE CHOICE FOR THE DEVELOPMENT OF AN ACTIVITY-BASED COSTING AND MANAGEMENT SYSTEM

Functionality

Maintenance

Links to other information systems

Cost

Flexibility

Organisational control

Skills

Functionality

As we have indicated there are a diversity of uses for activity-based costing information ranging from establishing a product profitability system to a system of activity-based budgeting. The detail and complication of the required system depends on the precise uses which are chosen for the system.

Maintenance

If one is to choose outside software, either for the whole software solution or as a basis for customisation, it is important to consider the software maintenance issues. Will the vendor company support the software? How reliable is their existence? Do they provide forums to discuss problems with other users? How will one relate to software updates? These are questions which need to be considered.

Links to other information systems

There will, in all probability, be a need to import information of a financial, transactions and activity statistics nature into the activity-based system. The ease with which this can be undertaken should be a criterion in judging the systems solution.

Cost

In considering the different systems' solutions their respective costs should be considered, not only in terms of the purchase costs of any software, but the hardware and development costs.

Flexibility

Although I have stressed that the best activity-based management projects depend on the detailed specification of the whole project requirements at the beginning of the project, the initial specification will not be perfect. If a new information system is being introduced to any organisation, the recipients of the new information will not be able, in advance, to specify the precise information which they require. When they receive the initial mock up of reports and the initial information it will lead them to ask better questions than they have been able to in the past. Good new information will allow them to learn in regards to understanding the problems of the organisation, this will lead them to formulate different information requirements. Thus systems flexibility is an important requirement in deciding on the systems solution to the project.

Organisational control

The control of systems is always an issue on any financial information project. If the project is to be flexible to the needs of the implementation team they have to control the systems development and usage. This may have implications for the software choice.

Skills

The project team will require some systems development skills if they are to have control of the systems solution. The nature of these skills should be reflected in the recruitment process for the team and the choice of system. If one employs a group of consultants it is important to ensure that they do not just import the software with which they are familiar since this may suit their requirements but not necessarily yours.

The choice of a systems solution is one of the early tasks which the project team should undertake since it can condition the ways in which the data is collected and there may have to be a process of systems development proceeding in tandem with the information gathering process.

THE OUTPUT OF THE ACTIVITY-BASED COSTING PROCESS

An overview of the output of the activity-based costing process is outlined in Figure 6.2. This is an attempt to specify the totality of information requirements, in any organisation there may only be a requirement for a subset of these requirements given the decision of how to implement activity-based management.

The specification of the outputs from an activity-based costing system will in part be a set of regular reports. These reports will have to be identified and a number of questions will have to be answered, in regards to: the level of reporting to be provided; a specification and definition of reporting units; the format of the report and the detail to be included; the frequency of reports and who should be the recipients. It is possible to generate a series of dummy reports for management at an early stage of the project, but one must bear in mind that these will command less management interest and attention than the first versions of the 'real thing', which are likely to lead to further changes and additional requests.

Figure 6.2
THE OUTPUT RANGE FROM AN ACTIVITY-BASED MANAGEMENT SYSTEM

Regular reports:	Products, distribution channels, customers, processes, etc.
Ad hoc information:	Used in the main as the basis for decision support systems but can also be used in operational systems.
Cost control information:	Cost analysis
Activity-based budgeting output:	Budgets, variance analysis, forecasts, etc.

There is a tendency for organisations to focus on regular reporting systems in the development of these types of projects. This is a major mistake and I will discuss the nature of the problems which are raised in the next chapter. One of the most central uses of the data is as an input into other systems be they decision support or operational. Any major organisational decision should be the subject of specific financial scrutiny and a key information database for this will be the activity-based costing database. The usage of this information, for example in evaluation of the financial impacts of launching a new product can be very useful. The information may also be used to input into operational systems, to take for example the decision in regards to credit scoring. Traditionally the decision whether to grant credit to an individual was based on the probability that the account will default, this can be augmented by a financial analysis of the impacts to cost and revenue of the account being successful or default, so a judgement on the 'cut off score' can be made on improved financial grounds.

The information required for cost reviews in terms of cost classification and its reporting can be generated by the activity-based costing system. This information can be generated to both suggest areas of concern in regards to costs and to monitor the degree to which any cost control programme has been successful.

The setting up of an activity-based budgeting process will most likely involve the revamping of the organisation's budgetary system. The new system will involve the predicting and monitoring of the levels of activity drivers and the generation of cost profiles both forecast and actual for individual cost centres and their budgetary line items. The system will have to be able to generate a variance analysis based on activity-based costing. This will also have to be related to the desired process of collection and dissemination of budgetary information.

THE ORGANISATIONAL IMPACTS OF ACTIVITY-BASED MANAGEMENT

Any serious attempt to introduce activity-based management in an organisation will have a very profound impact on the operations of that organisation. The strategy and product development process will be revolutionised, the monitoring and development of customer, product and distribution unit policy may be radically improved, the cost structure may be more sensibly controlled and the whole budgetary process can be greatly improved.

These changes will not happen unless there is a radical change in the way in which the organisation operates. The process recommended is one of a project in stages with each stage depending on the successful completion of the previous stage. This will lead to enhanced importance for the project only if it is seen to be sufficiently useful. It can prove to be an organisational revolution so it is important at each stage to produce results which are of a nature and quality so that the organisation buys the product.

CONCLUSIONS

This chapter has given an overview of the process by which activity-based costing and management can be introduced to an organisation. It is at a sufficiently high level of detail that one can perceive the main tasks to be undertaken, it is not a technical manual so that much of the detail on an individual project will have to be filled in. It is also important to note one of the themes of this chapter has been the need to decide for each organisation what is the menu of activity-based costing and management options which it wishes to implement. Since each organisation is unique it will require a unique development process and the system which is created will also be unique. The virtue of the technique is that it can cater individually to each and every organisation, however it should be cautioned that it requires care and subtlety to implement it properly. As with all management techniques they will only create value if implemented sensibly in the situation in which they are used.

7

Pitfalls in the development of activity-based management systems

INTRODUCTION

The introduction of activity-based management, like that of any other management technique, does not automatically ensure success. It can be implemented in a way which has an adverse impact to an organisation. There are dangers which must be guarded against. Cost reduction programmes, for example, may involve an organisation in very serious risk taking. I was very impressed by one management consultant who specialised in this type of programme and commented that cost reduction programmes usually obtained the level of cost savings for which they were targeted, however the implications were on occasions unacceptable to the organisation, in that they could very adversely impact staff morale and therefore operations. An effective cost reduction programme involves more than identifying the nature of cost savings, it requires a very careful attention to the impacts on human relations within the organisation. These issues go far beyond those raised by activity-based management. This chapter, however, will try to concentrate on some of the more likely problems and issues raised by introducing activity-based management to an organisation.

INSUFFICIENT ORGANISATIONAL COMMITMENT

A key point made throughout this book is the need for top management commitment as a prerequisite for the introduction of new management processes. There is always a problem that financial information and control systems will be subverted by the activities of other departments in serving their own interests. A common example of this type of problem relates to the capital appraisal process. Activity-based costing will aid in the forecasting of the cost and revenue structure of the organisation, this information will be an important input into any decision support modelling for the capital appraisal decision. In most large organisations expenditure on capital is the subject of a formal appraisal process. The formality of this process will often hide the fact that the key investment decisions are made on the basis of little effective financial analysis and the financial analysis is seen as a final hurdle to be overcome by a project. This may involve the political manipulation of the process. If there is an activity-based costing system with a high degree of accuracy, this will not enhance the validity of the capital appraisal process. Large expenditures may be made on whim with little analysis, planning or monitoring. An organisation is a number of different specialisms and cultures acting together and it will only be effective if they all contribute to a balanced perspective. Ensuring the effective use of activity-based costing information needs the custodians of the activity-based costing information to continually proselytise within the organisation. There are some roles that finance will find it easy to maintain, as for example, being the custodians of the budgetary process. In other roles they will probably have to convince their colleagues of the efficacy of the information which they can provide. There is a traditional conflict of culture, training and interest between the financial and marketing functions in any organisation. Activity-based costing information on product and customer profitability can be of great importance in improving the financial performance of the marketing function, but the marketers need to be convinced that financial information is useful. My personal experience of these problems is that one must try to develop mutually beneficial activities with all the different parts of the organisation; ensuring that project teams have representatives from all the interested parts of the organisation and explicitly have a finance officer who will be responsible for all the financial analysis to ensure that financial concerns are embedded in any project. One must be aware that most relationships are on-going and conflict where it is too extreme will only make relations on the next issue more difficult to sensibly manage. If there are major problems in the financial nature of decisions made by other departments then, *in extremis* the power of financial embarrassment – this decision is financially disastrous – will ensure in the long term intransigent positions are unlikely to be taken. Therefore although one tries to ensure the impact of activity-based management by insisting on the support of top management in setting up and managing its introduction, there will always be an on-going set of issues to ensure its influence is imbued in the management process. The full acceptance can certainly be helped by the way in which the project is set up and managed, but it is also an on-going process of developing organisational influence. A great pitfall is that an organisation spends resources on implementing such a project and then ignores the benefits which it can give to that organisation.

TOO MUCH ATTENTION TO REGULAR REPORTS

In considering the development of an activity-based costing system there is an inevitable focus on the precise nature of the system to be developed and the nature of any reports to be produced. The difficulty with regular reports is that they are often difficult to interpret. In my life as a corporate finance officer I was perpetually concerned with the possible interpretations which might be made in relation to any information that it was my responsibility to produce. This problem is particularly the case with regular reports. In systems development of activity-based costing systems, the focus can easily be monopolised by regular reports, the main issues in relation to suppliers of software are usually in terms of the structure of regular reports. If one focuses undue attention on regular reports one will miss what can be in operation the most important impact of activity-based costing information, in that, it allows a much higher quality of decision support information to be produced. Regular reports are invariably pictures of what has happened and they have to be drawn up on the basis of some arbitrary decisions as to what shall be included in the numbers. They are at best indicators of issues, problems and tentative decisions. They are too imprecise a tool to be used to indicate the appropriate action and should only be used for decisions which have small impacts or where there is not time or resource to produce more relevant information. It has always been my view that every important decision in an organisation requires specific financial analysis. This will ensure that the financial impacts are sensibly considered. A major benefit from the introduction of activity-based management should be in improving decision support. In designing any information gathering process and systems development the decision support requirements should be fully considered. There is an undoubted tendency for projects to overlook these requirements.

UNDERSTANDING COSTS

Activity-based costing is, in essence, a technique which enables an organisation to better understand how its cost structure behaves. If it has a purpose, that is it, expressed in its simplest terms. Put in this way it allows one to highlight some of its likely limitations as a technique. If one considers the way in which costs were discussed in Chapter 5, they were allocated to activities and then to cost objects like products and customers via the volume of activity drivers. If activities were not related to, in this instance, products or customers, they would be classified as overheads. The interesting issue is that where they are related to products they may, by implication, be seen as being variable. In the standard analysis of activity-based costing the distinction between fixed and variable costs plays a singularly background role. The activity-based costs are sometimes seen as long term variable costs. If, for example, one is setting up an activity-based budgeting system, then one derives activity rates by dividing the total cost of an activity by the volume of the relevant activity driver and then determines the budget by multiplying the activity rate by the expected volume of the activity driver. This is a judgement as to which costs are variable. One of my worries about the technique is that these judgements will be imported uncritically into the activity-based management process. The difficulties which can arise from these implicit assumptions are illustrated in Figure 7.1.

Figure 7.1 depicts the average cost per unit of an activity driver in a particular department which undertakes a single activity. We are considering two different cost structures, A and B. The average cost structure represented by A is where the department total cost is fixed

Figure 7.1
THE BEHAVIOUR OF COSTS

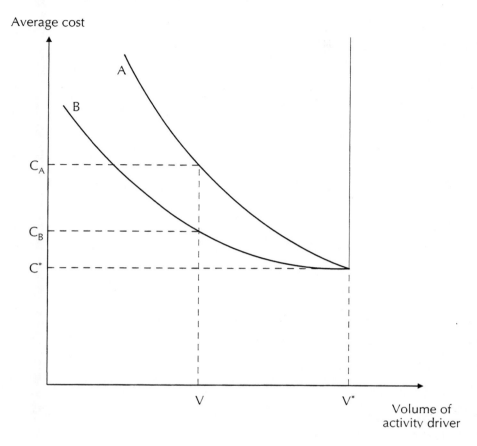

irrespective of volume and that represented by B shows total cost
increasing with volume. The type of department might be one related
to credit card processing at a particular bank, in the case of A the
staffing levels are fixed irrespective of volume and for B there would
be a range of staff whose employment depends on the levels of
processing volumes. This type of operation is common to all types of
organisation. The costs become vertical at V^* since that is the
maximum capacity of the organisational unit, driven perhaps by some
technological constraint. The activity in the department is related to
both products and customers and so is included as part of product and
customer profitability analysis. The information gathering process takes
place when the volume of the activity driver is V. If the cost structure is
represented by A then the estimated activity cost will be C_A and if the

costs are represented by B then the estimated activity costs will be C_B. Where these costs are used to analyse the impact of volume changes they will lead to errors in the cost levels. If, for example, the forecast level of activity driver used as part of the budgetary process is V^* then the costs should be C^*, using C_A or C_B will be in error.

Figure 7.2
COST CLASSIFICATION

Directly variable costs

Managerially variable costs

Cost object fixed costs

Overheads

The central issue is being able to understand the actual behaviour of costs at the level of individual organisational units. The factors which determine the variability of costs in my experience relate to the technology of the activity in a department, the length of time one is considering – the longer the time period the more likely that costs will be variable – and the way in which the unit is managed. The introduction of activity-based management will help to variabilise the costs. In general terms it is better for an organisation if it can make more costs variable since it reduces the risks to the organisation originating from changes in the levels of activity volumes. In analysing the costs of a department I have found it useful to use the classification of costs depicted in Figure 7.2. Directly variable costs would be costs which vary directly with volume, material input costs would be a good example of this. Managerially variable costs would be costs which do not automatically vary with volume but can be volume related provided that there is an appropriate managerial decision, the laying off of staff when business is slack would relate to an example of this type of cost. Cost object related fixed costs are costs which tend not to relate to volumes of cost objects like products but which can be associated with those objects. If a particular product is the subject of a marketing campaign, the campaign will not be product volume related, but the cost can be associated with a product. Overheads are costs which are unrelated to the volumes of the cost object being considered. Considering the way in which costs are determined will aid in the development of decision support information and the application of cost control and activity-based budgeting.

ALLOCATING COSTS

One of the more frequent questions asked in relation to activity-based costing systems is how one should allocate costs. The initial literature on activity-based costing focused on the non-allocation of overheads to cost objects, like customers or products. There are in essence two types of issues which relate to this; 'should one produce regular reported numbers on a marginal or fully absorbed basis?' and 'what should one do with particular types of costs, as for example, information technology costs?' There is in my view no entirely satisfactory answer to these questions, there are however a number of ideas which are helpful in putting these questions into context.

Decision support

Regular reports have to be drawn up on the basis of some arbitrary decisions and should be used to have a broad overview of organisational performance. They can never be exactly related to an individual decision. Decision support information can be customised.

Appropriate for purpose

The decisions as to which costs should be included or excluded should depend on one's expectations of the uses to which the information will be put. If one is an organisation considering customer profitability, for example, then one might be interested in customer groups or individual customers. If there are large numbers of customers some costs will not vary with an addition of an extra customer but would vary if the customer based varied by 1000 customers. These costs might be included if the decisions are to be made in terms of large numbers of customers and excluded if one is looking at customers on an individual basis.

Information transparency

A problem which leads to the misuse of information is where the composition of the numbers is not understood by those using the information. The proper transparent expression of the information will help to minimise this problem. I am always tempted to advise, that drawing up numbers with enhanced information will allow users to make their own adjustments to data to suit their purposes.

Sophistication of users

The level of financial sophistication of the recipients of information should influence the nature of the information produced within an organisation. There should also be a continual process of education for the management so that sensible interpretations are made of the information.

The questions relate to how likely it is that information will lead to poor decisions. It is difficult to decide in general terms what is the correct response to these issues. In general it is sensible to draw up the regular reports so that any allocations of costs which are not directly variable are transparent from the perspectives of the users.

THE INFORMATION GATHERING PROCESS

The quality of the information gathering process underpins the success of activity-based management. If the information gathered is not appropriate for its uses or insufficient then any policies or decisions based on that information may lead to mistakes. Thus this process should be the subject of the greatest degree of care and scrutiny. This point has already been stressed in considering the motivation of an activity-based management project.

THE USE OF CONSULTANTS

Most businesses have an ambivalent attitude towards consultants. They undoubtedly have a set of interests which can be at variance to that of the organisation in which they work. They will wish to apply their methodologies, however, provided that they are sensibly selected, they do have experience and insight which can be highly valuable. They need to be managed positively and effectively and they can provide value to the project.

CONCLUSIONS

The success of an activity-based management project depends heavily on ensuring its implementation reflects the unique nature of your organisation. It is a political process and will require an implementation which is organisationally specific. In technical terms it is vital to ensure the information is fit for the purpose for which it is collected and that it provides a good understanding of how the costs of the organisation actually behave. It will then enable a better understanding of how the organisation's financial results are obtained and how they can be improved. No implementation is easy even from a technical perspective and requires subtlety and creativity.

Part 4

Conclusions

8

Conclusions

Balanced scorecards and activity-based management have been the two most important developments in management accounting during the past twenty years. They have enabled organisations to better understand what goals they are trying to achieve and how they are trying to achieve those goals. They enable the setting up of a management system which will improve the quality with which the organisation is managed. The resulting management information system will be catered directly to the needs of the organisation.

The balanced scorecard focuses on the strategy of the organisation and enables financial indicators to be put within a more integrated framework where one can understand policy and success from a coherent overall perspective. It is an extremely powerful management tool.

Activity-based management enables an organisation to better understand and manage its financial results. It will enhance the profitability and value of any commercial organisation.

Taken together these techniques should revolutionise the strategic, budgetary, planning and decision making processes of the organisation and be a key tool from which all organisational managers can benefit. The techniques are, in principle, applicable to any type of organisation.